Untangling Whiteness

Education, Resistance and Transformation

by
Jennifer Gale de Saxe
Victoria University of Wellington

Series in Sociology

VERNON PRESS

www.vernonpress.com

In the Americas:
Vernon Press
1000 N West Street, Suite 1200
Wilmington, Delaware, 19801
United States

In the rest of the world:
Vernon Press
C/Sancti Espiritu 17,
Malaga, 29006
Spain

Series in Sociology

Library of Congress Control Number: 2024938929

ISBN: 979-8-8819-0113-4

Also available: 979-8-8819-0043-4 [Hardback]; 979-8-8819-0091-5 [PDF, E-Book]

Cover design by Vernon Press. Illustration by Dr Bonnie-Estelle Trotter-Simons.

Table of Contents

Acknowledgements

There are many people who have been part of my teaching, learning, writing, brainstorming, and editing of this book. To Dr Adele Norris: Thank you for all the conversations, guest lecturing, co-presenting, and co-writing over the last few years. Your intellectual contribution to the book and my teaching and learning has been and will continue to be invaluable for both me and my students. To Dr Dyan Watson: Your chapter, *Staying in the Conversation*, is the inspiration for one of the most powerful writing assignments I ask students to engage in. The ethos and philosophy of your chapter have helped me to create a safe and academically challenging space to teach and learn at the university. Thank you for being a model educator for me. To Dr Lorena Gibson: Thank you for all the conversations about our teaching and shared research interests. Your commitment to thinking outside the box about your teaching, learning, and assessments is inspiring. To Dr Alain Sykes: Thank you for keeping our intellectual conversations alive as you move all around the world. I can't wait to co-present again someday. To Dr Eli Elinoff and Dr Liam Martin: Thank you both for your open ears, and advice throughout the book writing, editing, researching, drafting processes. Your feedback and insight have been more helpful than you might know. To Dr Liana MacDonald: Thank you for the conversations about our shared teaching, pedagogy and learning interests. Your scholarship has added so much to the development of this book, as well as helped me to situate the theoretical content here in Aotearoa. To Dr Nayantara Sheoran Appleton: Thank you for always being available to work through the most abstract to the most mundane ideas and thoughts. To Dr Dave Wilson: Thank you for always being up for a writing session for this book… which only sometimes stayed on course as a writing session. Thank you to Dr Bambi Cheva-Isarakul, Dr Corrina Howland, Jaymee Lundin, and Dr Grant Otsuki for your continued support and for reading through and editing multiple iterations of the book chapters. To Dr Caroline Bennett, Dr Kevin Dew, Dr Chamsy el-Ojeili, and Dr Jack Foster: Thank you for your various contributions of support throughout the book proposal stage. To Dr Jacs Forde: Thank you for all those writing sessions and for listening to all the minutia that comes with the final stages of the book writing and editing processes. To Danielle Hanna, Alex Ker, and Dr Bonnie-Estelle Trotter-Simons: Thank you for teaching, tutoring, lecturing, writing, and working with me. The last seven years of teaching at VUW would not be possible without the care, insight, and generosity you bring into the classroom community. I am a better teacher and learner because of you three. I also thank my spouse and kids, Brent, Ben, Sam, and Leah and your unrelenting support in the writing of this book. I know that too many times I brought my work home and talked about it too much, but you all continue to support me by listening to stories about my teaching, what I learn from my students, and all the other things that come with writing a book. Finally, I acknowledge and dedicate this book to my students, as they have been teaching and learning with me for over two decades. There are so many stories, ideas, lessons, discussions, projects, and conversations that I've had with students over the years. I feel fortunate and privileged to have taught and learned with so many passionate individuals. Thank you for contributing and being instrumental in my growth and development as a teacher and lifelong learner.

Introduction

I am a lifelong teacher and learner, and have taught for almost three decades in the primary and secondary years, community college, and universities. I taught at a private school, underfunded and risk-of-closing public schools in three US states, a small liberal arts college, and large public universities in both the United States and Aotearoa, New Zealand. What I have come to understand in all of these teaching roles is that learning from and with students is the only way education is truly meaningful and has the potential to be life-changing and liberatory. No one (educators or students) comes into a classroom community objectively or without life experiences. Everyone understands concepts differently and learns in diverse ways. We all have varied racialised experiences, come from diverse socio-economic backgrounds, participate in multi-faceted religious and political education, as well as embody different ways that we understand our roles and purposes in the world. In other words, teaching and learning are steeped in subjectivity, diversity, and interconnectivity.

I identify and have been socialised as a white, able-bodied, heterosexual, cisgender, middle-class Jewish, European American female who lives and teaches sociology and social policy in the settler colonial country of Aotearoa, New Zealand. My complexity as a human being is instrumental in how I engage in any form of learning and teaching. The lens of resistance I connect and work to embody is the global movement to challenge and undermine white supremacy. Contextually, I situate my teaching and learning is the university classroom; spaces that are often tense and are currently challenged around the world. Most important, I write this book as a way to directly interrogate the assumption that teaching and learning about race and whiteness, particularly within the university context, can be condensed to one course, one workshop, or even a few trainings. It is a life-long process of learning that may begin in one university classroom, but must continue as part of who I am as an unfinished and undetermined being. I understand that every reader of this book is on their own path of untangling theories of race and whiteness. Thus, the theories and concepts will resonate in particular and unique ways depending on upbringing, education, experience, and levels of comfort/discomfort when discussing and learning about such content.

Untangling and interrogating racism and whiteness are context and content-specific. Although a definitional or descriptive understanding may be a good starting point for learning about them as concepts, the way they manifest is very much socially constructed and intertwined with the history, culture and politics of ones' social and geographic location. I unpack many concepts as they relate to race and whiteness at length throughout the book, but for the purpose of grounding ones' thinking from the outset, I briefly define a few key terms so that readers can situate and make sense of them from here on. These definitions are just the starting point for what will be intricately fleshed out and discussed within the book. I have chosen four specific terms that are used often in each chapter. There is some overlap in ideas throughout the four terms, as they feed into and rely upon one another in their manifestations and how they are actualised individually, structurally, and institutionally. After these brief descriptions, I provide a short discussion of how whiteness and race are situated and conceptualised in Aotearoa, New Zealand, the country in which I currently live and teach.

Whiteness: Whiteness is understood as a default status or descriptor as it occupies a space as 'normal' and 'neutral.' It is seen as 'raceless' and 'clear.' Whiteness also relies on how it is socially constructed within a society that positions people the highest (idealised) on a racial hierarchy, as well as whom on the racial hierarchy are considered 'white' at any given point in time as well as ones' geographic location. For example, Jewish, Italian, and Irish people in the United States in the early 20th century were considered not-white. Whiteness is a concept of interworking and interconnecting practices and meanings that reinforce a dominant position of racial formation.

White Supremacy: White supremacy as a term is often equated with physical violence and horrific, unspeakable brutality from groups intent on reinforcing the supremacy of the 'white race'. I do not refute this definition, but extend its meaning throughout the book to include other forms of violence and harm through a *system,* a *matrix,* and a *web* that reinforces and upholds racial power and privilege as it manifests through its practices, policies, philosophies, etc. This harm is maintained and sustained through the suppression, dehumanisation, and marginalisation of Black, Indigenous and People of Colour (BIPOC).[1] By extending the definition of white supremacy, it becomes more difficult for white people to abdicate the responsibility of reaping the benefits of being part of a system that privileges them whilst suppressing and harming other.

---

[1] In this book I use BIPOC to acknowledge the racial and ethnic diversity within marginalised communities.

Race: Race is understood as a classification system that is based on phenotypical characteristics. In addition to race being based on physical appearances, it is also very much socially constructed, relying on stereotypes and assumptions within a racial hierarchy that are specific to ones' social and geographic location. 'Having race' is often framed and understood as only for those who are considered 'not white,' or for racialised 'Others'. Whiteness is seen as opaque (hence, without race) in its hegemonically (often not questioned) agreed-upon societal definition. The social construction of one's race can also be seen and understood by how someone is racially defined in one geographic location (Person of Colour) but is racially defined differently in another geographic location ('no race' or white). Further, the way one racially self-identifies may be different to the race they are ascribed by others.

Racism: Racism is an individual, structural, and institutional philosophy, presence, and practice that is intimately connected to the essence of how a society functions and behaves. Racial groups are hierarchically ordered in relation to their proximity to whiteness. For this reason, in order to uphold racism, (in its many manifestations), there must be an agreed-upon understanding to how whiteness is positioned on the racial hierarchy. This hierarchy is directly connected to social positioning and practices that esteem the superiority of whiteness. Racism is the active behaviour, policies, and practices that manifest in regard to ones' racial categorisation. Racism is also subtle and covert in that it relies on philosophies that are deeply steeped in structures and institutions that uphold and prioritise whiteness whilst demeaning and dehumanising groups and individuals who are not white.

Although brief, these definitions begin the process of grounding and understanding the many theories, ideas, and concepts that interconnect and rely upon one another to uphold and sustain the whiteness of the university and society writ-large. What follows is a short discussion of how whiteness is understood, discussed, and actualised in Aotearoa, New Zealand.

Whiteness in Aotearoa New Zealand[2]

Though a detailed history of whiteness in Aotearoa, New Zealand, is beyond the scope of this introduction, it is important to briefly contextualise it so that readers may better understand what I refer to when discussing the importance of context, location and/or geographic location in terms of how whiteness

---

[2] Elements of this section are drawn from (Norris, de Saxe, & Cooper, 2023)

operationalises in education and society. As Elers and Jayan (2020) note, "[W]hiteness continues to mark itself as an invisible standard through which racialised others are measured" (pp. 238-239). Whiteness, through the very act of being 'unseen' itself, can silence and erase BIPOC experiences and worldviews, thereby enabling white supremacy. This process is evident in Aotearoa, whereby whiteness is upheld by the enduring impacts of European colonisation of Māori, the indigenous peoples of Aotearoa. As Azarmandi (2022) argues,

> Race as an idea has enabled the complex racial formations and projects that have worked overtime to reproduce race-based power structures that in Aotearoa New Zealand privilege and benefit Pākehā,[3] primarily through dispossession of the Indigenous people in the process of colonisation (p.134)

Throughout many of the chapters, I draw on seminal Māori scholar and activist Awatare and her book *Māori Sovereignty*. Published in 1986, it was and is a ground-breaking analysis of conceptualising whiteness in Aotearoa. Awatare argues that white systems determine the limits by which Māori can, in fact, govern Māori, illustrating the omnipresent nature of whiteness. Its power lies in the normalcy and invisibility of whiteness, which engenders white supremacy that has largely been under-theorised in Aotearoa, New Zealand.[4] Awatere's analysis of Māori initial encounters with British forces is often discussed from the position of Māori mass dispossession that led to generations of deprivation. Donna Awatere's astute attention toward the institutionalisation of the white body has received less attention, but nonetheless is crucial to understanding the forces Māori encounter in pursuit of self-determination. Whiteness could not have accrued the level of perpetual benefits without a sustained focus on Māori as being a problem, or problem people (see Gordon, 2013). Awatere's attention here is similar to the question W.E.B. DuBois posed in 1903: What does it mean to be a problem? DuBois, as Gordon (2013) notes, does not speak about being Black but rather its meaning, which demarcates the line between identity and

---

[3] Pākehā is the Māori word for white New Zealanders of European descent.

[4] There was certainly a rich oral tradition that was acutely aware of what I am referring to as white systems and imperialism. From very early on Māori developed a nuanced understanding and awareness of what whiteness represented and how it was operationalised. Such an awareness is best seen in the teachings, songs and prophecies of leaders like Kingi Tawhiao, Te Kooti Rikirangi. See Judith Binney's (2012) historical biography of the life of Te Kooti Rikirangi called *Redemption Songs*.

liberation. Identity, as described by Gordon (2013), "calls for the question of a being's relationship with itself," and liberation is concerned with questions of 'ought' and 'why': Who is to be liberated? (p. 65).

The ways that British colonisers positioned Anglo-centric ideals and knowledge in Aotearoa as superior to tikanga me te ao Māori (Māori culture and worldview) forced many Māori to assimilate to Pākehā values, thus dispossessing them of land, culture and language (Came-Friar et al., 2019). Subsequent breaches of Te Tiriti o Waitangi, (the Treaty of Waitangi; the founding document between Māori and the British Crown in Aotearoa),[5] and a misremembering of the country's history of colonisation (Jackson, 2019), continue to have negative effects on Māori communities and other communities of colour. Understanding the operations of whiteness and racism in Aotearoa New Zealand can help to make sense of the inequities between Māori and Pākehā that are evident across social determinants (Bécares, Cormack & Harris, 2013; Harris et al., 2006).

One way that whiteness and institutional racism are brushed under the rug is through Aotearoa's focus on being a 'bicultural' nation. In fact, this narrative is often disseminated around the globe, even claiming that Aotearoa has some of the best race relations in the world (Richards, 2020; Stewart, 2023). However, espousing biculturalism without confronting and dismantling tropes and stereotypes used to justify Māori continued oppression and dispossession is a continuation of the colonial project. Awatere argues that stereotypes of the 'Māori heathen' and 'savage' never vanished but strengthened under white colonial systems of confinement. Savages, Awatere writes, morphed into Māori as 'troublemakers,' 'ethnic parasites, and 'burden to white taxpayers' (p. 19). The creation of tropes plays out significantly in the gatekeeping systems: housing, education, employment, and criminal justice. Privileging whiteness and reinforcing racial domination strengthened over time through the persistence of negative stereotypes and prejudices among members of the core structure that cultivated a racially discriminatory consciousness that has both placed Māori in a permanent state of disadvantage and white people in a perpetual state of ignorance–oblivious to the institutionalisation of white supremacy. Notably, "white people have no real identity of their own apart from that which exists through opposition to the Māori" (Awatare, p.11). These

---

[5] For more information about Te Tiriti o Waitangi, see *Te Tiriti o Waitangi* (Orange, 2012).

examples illustrate, for Awatere, a system operating effectively under a white supremacist system.

Through my observations and experiences living in Aotearoa for the past several years, I notice a general discomfort among people when talking about race and white supremacy in the context of Aotearoa and its history. For example, Stewart (2020) observes that "[R]acism" is a dirty word and a grave insult in Aotearoa, New Zealand, and many Pākehā react with anger if anyone raises the question of racism. As Azarmandi (2022) notes, whiteness and Pākehāness are not sufficiently problematised. In fact, there is often more of a focus on representation and belonging rather than a dismantling of the structures that have positioned certain identity groups as superior in a settler-colonial system. Additionally, though the education systems in Aotearoa are increasingly recognising race as a systemic construct that can be 'untaught,' (e.g. Teaching Council of Aotearoa New Zealand, 2021; Ministry of Education, 2022), whiteness still manifests in inequitable outcomes between Māori and Pākehā students, as well as other minoritised ethnic groups. For example, whiteness operates in teachers' deficit framing of Māori students' academic achievement, (Bishop et al., 2003) and through the greater educational capital and mobility Pākeha middle-class students tend to have due to historic privilege (Borell et al., 2018). Students who learn in education systems that centre Pākehā worldviews generally have fewer opportunities and experiences to learn in culturally responsive environments; consequently, these systems reinforce values and attitudes that centre and privilege whiteness and settler colonialism.

In an interview in June 2021, Chris Hipkins, Aotearoa's former Prime Minister (and former Education Minister), responded to a question about proposed secondary school curriculum changes by claiming that the term white privilege "generates a reaction from people that actually puts up a barrier to them genuinely engaging in a conversation about power imbalance" (Satherly, 2021). I presume people in Aotearoa generally avoid using terms such as 'white privilege' and race, as they are considered confrontational and divisive, thus using 'ethnicity' instead. However, the ways people use and relate to these terms undoubtedly differ depending on individuals' racial standpoint and positionality, as well as their comfort level and experience in discussing race and whiteness.

I present this short description of whiteness in Aotearoa, New Zealand, so that readers can understand the importance of context, history, and geographic location when learning and engaging critical theories of race and whiteness.

Although many of the scholars and concepts I draw from throughout the book come from a North American or British context, their meanings provide a useful framework and lens in which to untangle, make sense of, and analyse whiteness and how it is upheld and reproduced in Aotearoa New Zealand. These same theories and concepts can also be used as tools of disruption and resistance for actively working toward challenging and undermining racism and white supremacy. The importance of socially, geographically, historically, and politically situating oneself whilst reading the book is vital when working to move away from proclamations that white supremacy and racism aren't as bad as they are 'over there.' In fact, when I first started teaching courses in Aotearoa, many students would often proudly state, "At least things in NZ aren't as bad as they are in the United States". It becomes too easy to make such claims when diving into theory that originates in other parts of the world, and specifically discusses and situates the discussion 'over there.' I circle back to learning these ideas and theories as frameworks and lenses that can be used to make sense of something. Although the details and histories might differ, the language deployed to understand an idea is still applicable when working towards making sense of it at the individual, systemic, and institutional level. Thus, before reading on, I ask readers to orient themselves and take a moment to consider the context and geographic location of where they are so that each chapter resonates socially, politically, historically, and geographically.

Foreword

George Yancy

I have had the experience of reading texts that communicate a deep sense of *urgency*. They not only touch me conceptually but imbue me with a sense of resolution, especially when there is so much that is politically and existentially at stake. Such texts require that all of us remain steadfast as we bear witness to their deeply uncomfortable themes, as we refuse to look away, and as we allow the full weight of their message to unsettle us. Jennifer de Saxe's brave, thought-provoking, and insightful text, *Untangling Whiteness: Education, Resistance, and Transformation*, is written with that deep sense of urgency, verve, and commitment. The text critically and astutely conceptualizes theory and praxis through a Freirean pedagogical lens. On this score, de Saxe's text is invitational, placing emphasis on critical and collective dialogue. The text encourages its readers not to retreat from facing hard truths about whiteness, but to speak out courageously against whiteness. Paulo Freire (2005) writes, "Human beings are not built in silence, but in word, in work, in action-reflection" (p. 88). In this sense, de Saxe's text is critical of forms of speech that are hegemonically designed to silence, to stifle our collective capacity to name and to embody freedom and transformation.

As I read through de Saxe's indispensable text, I quickly discerned its relentless drive to lay bare the complexity of whiteness. Within the context of whiteness, the act of "laying bare" is consistent with the project of exposing dominant structures that attempt to cover over or conceal their violent machinations and regimes of oppression. de Saxe *unpacks/untangles* important theories, definitions, and concepts regarding whiteness and race. I read her text as also *unpacking/untangling* the knot of whiteness. After all, the structure of whiteness, as de Saxe unflaggingly demonstrates, is insidious and attempts to obfuscate its violence and its hegemony through processes of normalization. Whiteness possesses, as de Saxe argues, a default status, which also functions as a site of evasion. Naming and identifying the ways in which whiteness remains hidden in its veneer of normalization is extremely important because whiteness functions as the transcendental norm. By that I mean that whiteness possesses the power to appear "unraced" and yet produces "racial differences." In this way, whiteness acquires a sense of invisibility and deceptively constructs itself as human *tout court*. As Michael W. Apple (1991) writes, "White people usually are not seen and named. They are centered as the human norm. 'Others' are raced; 'we' are just people" (p. 10). On this score, Black people, Indigenous people, and People of Color (BIPOC) are deemed "sub-persons," "sub-humans," "savages" and "bestial." Hence, as the transcendental norm, whiteness possesses the requisite discursive, material, and institutional power to construct a metanarrative that underwrites and reinforces the "superiority" of whiteness as "natural," as "the axiomatic apex of civilization," as "manifest destiny."

In unpacking and untangling the structure of whiteness, de Saxe is sensitive to the context and locationality of how whiteness manifests and operationalizes itself in both education and society. This approach is significant as whiteness is not simply an intramural phenomenon. It isn't marginal or episodic in its violence. Rather, whiteness is systemically and pervasively violent throughout societies and polities structured by its overt and covert logics. In short, de Saxe demonstrates that whiteness is not just a case of nation building; it is a process "where," in DuBoisian terms, "whiteness is the ownership of the earth forever and ever, Amen!" (DuBois, 1995, p. 454). As Charles Mills (1997) states, "White supremacy is the unnamed political system that has made the modern world what it is today" (p. 1). de Saxe's critical awareness of the ways in which whiteness manifests itself contextually and globally places important responsibility on white people, that is, those who benefit from white privilege (etymologically, *privus lex* or private law). In this way, de Saxe courageously theorizes the reality of white complicity. There is, in short, no "white innocence." To be white is to be embedded within structures of white power and white supremacy, structures that make white privilege possible and that correspondingly disadvantage BIPOC, leaving them in unlivable states of social precarity.

Many white people tend to restrict white supremacy to those white supremacist groups that are overtly violent and express hatred toward BIPOC. In pointing the finger at such groups, it is easy for whiteness to bifurcate into "bad whites" and "good whites." This distinction, however, fails to capture the ways in which to be white is to be systemically ensconced in perpetuating whiteness as a structure of violence and otherization. The process of *untangling* whiteness refuses to facilitate the dynamics of bad faith, where white people deny or flee their complicity vis-à-vis whiteness. In our contemporary moment, we see this form of bad faith where white people claim to be "victims" of those groups who have historically experienced racialized systemic discrimination, policing, colonization, and violence. As such, those who have been and continue to be terrorized by whiteness are defined as "problem people" or as ontological problems, where their *being* is construed as a problem. de Saxe, however, argues that it is within a white racist world that white people are problems. Evading this truth helps whiteness to maintain its "invisibility," "center," and "innocence" and thereby creates the fiction that BIPOC are "inferior." Indeed, as a binary structure, whiteness parasitically thrives upon what it has created as the racialized other; indeed, it needs the fictional status of racialized others for its own fictional (white) identity. In this regard, whiteness is a site of production and consumption. Whiteness produces racialized fictions (Black people as violent, Indigenous peoples as savages and uncivilized, Asians as the Yellow Peril) only to consume those fictions as objects of fear and dread, which then function recursively to construct whiteness as law and order—the *master* of racialized "chaos."

de Saxe is aware of how whiteness surreptitiously recenters itself (intentionally or unintentionally). Through emphasis placed upon self-reflexivity and positionality, de Saxe understands the importance of thematizing the various ways in which we are positioned and socially constructed. Regarding white people, the process of self-criticality begins from a place of awareness of one's investment in whiteness, and how whiteness shapes one's *lived* experiences and social motility-in-the-world. Naming her intersectional identity (white, heterosexual, cisgender, able-bodied, and middle-class Jewish European American female, and as a person who lives and teaches sociology and social policy in the settler colonial country of Aotearoa New Zealand), de Saxe reveals how she embodies various identificatory registers that have meaning within a matrix of power relationships that have deep and important implications for the social, political, and existential trajectory of her life. If we are to take power structures seriously, we must be prepared to name who we are, where we stand, and face the processes of interpellation that will impact us. Given the focal point of whiteness within her text, de Saxe appropriately begins with her whiteness. To name the positionality of her whiteness implies both processes of self-interrogation and epistemic humility. As white, de Saxe understands the importance of rendering visible her own whiteness, and the importance of recognizing how being white can easily recenter itself in the form of white guilt, the good white, the heroic white, the white savior figure, the confessional white, and the expert white, especially regarding the topic of whiteness. These are processes that can easily function to privilege white modes of performance and white domination.

Racialized as Black and as a philosopher who understands and interrogates the structural anti-Blackness of whiteness within the US, I have witnessed white people, especially white students, avoid naming their whiteness or tarrying with their whiteness. Teaching at a Predominantly White Institution (PWI), I recall an experience when I was teaching a course I regularly teach entitled "Basic Problems of Philosophy." Halfway through the course, I had my students immerse themselves in critical readings on the theme of whiteness. Not surprisingly, many students found (and continue to find) it hard to believe that questions of race, racism, and whiteness qualify as specifically philosophical problems. This, of course, is partly a function of the whiteness of the field. By focusing on whiteness, my students, especially my white students, come to understand that philosophy is not reducible to a realm of abstract reflection, but dwells within the space of the quotidian, the everydayness of embodied life. As we delved into the heart of whiteness, one white male student asked me: "Haven't we discussed whiteness long enough?" I was taken aback as we had only considered whiteness for a relatively short period of time. My sense is that his aim, whether he was aware of it or not, was to belittle the complexity and structural violence of whiteness, and to deflect the pedagogical critical gaze away from whiteness, *his whiteness.* I communicated that the problem of whiteness is something that he would have to explore for the rest of his life. If I could speak to him today, I would add that the problem of whiteness will continue to exist well beyond his life and that as he approaches the end of his life, the opacity and complexity of whiteness will perdure. My point here is not to suggest that whiteness is a permanent feature of our social and political world. Rather, my point is that white people are psychically *invested* in whiteness; that their being depends upon the power, privilege, and normativity that whiteness affords. To divest fully from whiteness would involve a radical form of kenosis (or emptying)—the loss of whiteness as such.

This white male student treated whiteness as a superficial puzzle, as something that once completed, he could then move on from. It was as if he thought that he could unlearn whiteness in a single classroom session. I said to him, and by extension to the entire class, that whiteness is not a conceptual puzzle; it is not about mastery. My observations here are consistent with de Saxe's profound pedagogical insights where she is suspicious of white people who treat the process of "doing the work" of anti-racism as a checklist or as a one-off activity. It was as if he thought himself capable of autonomously disarticulating his whiteness from the pervasive material and discursive historicity of whiteness. His approach to whiteness was a modality of what de Saxe refers to as neoliberal racism. He saw himself as capable of extricating himself from the larger, extramural racial and racist processes of societal inequity/injustice caused by systemic white power and privilege. Seduced and shaped by an ontology of neoliberalism, most of my white students see themselves as atomic, *asocial* subjects. Part of the objective of the course was to expose them to an understanding of whiteness as heteronomous, as an expansive web of white discursive and nondiscursive power relations that are haptic, that is, that violently *touch* the lives of those who are not white. When open, my white students begin to see themselves as racially entangled in/with the lives of BIPOC. I explain to them that to acquire a critical understanding of the problematic nature of such a racial entanglement requires a profound shift in their understanding of who they are *as white* and a profound recognition that they have failed or refused to confront the toxicity of their whiteness and its deleterious impact on BIPOC.

I find that de Saxe's pedagogically engaging text functions as a powerful analysis of the complexities regarding teaching critical theories of race and whiteness. Furthermore, I find her delineation of various forms of resistance that are necessary to challenge whiteness both macroscopically and microscopically to be generative. I also find it essential to note that what pedagogically fuels this text is that de Saxe was motivated to write it based upon a sociology course, "Complicating Resistance: Sociology and Transformation," that she teaches in her current academic institution in Aotearoa, New Zealand. Hence, the text itself grows out of the actual daring to name whiteness within an academic institution situated within the context of Aotearoa's history of white hegemonic settler colonialism. I applaud de Saxe not only for writing this book, but for providing readers with an analysis of whiteness that speaks to the specificity of its configuration within that colonized space and for revealing the overlapping and shared global features of whiteness. Whether in the US or Aotearoa, de Saxe doesn't waste time debating whether toxic whiteness exists. She begins with that truth and invites us (*all of us*) as readers to critically come to terms with how we participate in upholding systems (plural) of oppression. In this way, de Saxe takes seriously the theory of intersectionality that focuses on multiple forms of oppression and marginalization. In other words, de Saxe is sensitive to the ways in which various identity markers (race, gender, sex, class, ability, culture, and so on) reveal different ways of experiencing the world and resisting imbricated oppressive structures.

Given my own *lived* experience as a Black person in the US, one who teaches and writes about and against whiteness, I find de Saxe's pedagogy regarding whiteness and resistance to it is a core and salient aspect of her text. Whiteness needs its other. As argued earlier, whiteness, as a social ontological binary structure, both produces and consumes its racial/racist caricatures and fictions. This is what whiteness does as it expands across the Atlantic, enslaving Black bodies or building white supremacist colonies in Aotearoa and beyond. As Albert Memmi (2000) writes, "The [white] racist ascribes to his victim a series of surprising traits, calling him incomprehensible, impenetrable, mysterious, strange, disturbing, and so on. Slowly he makes of his victim a sort of animal, a thing, or simply a symbol" (p. 176). On this score, to be racialized as Black within the US involved and involves being subjected to the white gaze, which is procrustean, hegemonic, and dehumanizing. To be Black is to be "fixed" by the white gaze, which is fueled by the white imaginary. Hence, to be Black is to be perceived as a site of "criminality," "hypersexuality," "inferiority," and, paradoxically, at times both "revolting" and "irresistible." White supremacy, as an unnamed/unmarked political system, is a process of white *worlding*. In that process of worlding, which involves white embodied practices that constantly generate racist tropes and semiotic constructions, one *becomes* white. It also involves, as Mills (1997) argues, "A cognitive model that precludes self-transparency and genuine understanding of social realities" (p. 18). In short, white people live according to an inverted epistemology that has "*the ironic outcome that* [they] *will in general be unable to understand the world they themselves have made*" (Mills, 1997, p. 18). This ironic outcome is a function of what Mills coined as an epistemology of ignorance, which is prescribed by the Racial Contract and frames and "justifies" the social, political, ontological, and axiological racial distortions regarding those who are not white.

Under white colonial violence in Aotearoa, de Saxe writes about how the Māori people were stereotyped as "heathens" and "savages" and how these derogatory terms continue to degrade, only now referring to them as "troublemakers," or "burdens on white taxpayers." Think here of the racist stereotype of the Black "welfare queen," along with the implications of "laziness" and "irresponsibility." In both the US context and within the context of Aotearoa, what it means to be white is defined through what it is *not*. This raises the issue, of which de Saxe is aware, of what the meaning of whiteness is apart from its racialized other. In short, it leaves one to wonder if whiteness is anything at all other than what it projects. It is important to note that de Saxe makes it clear that as in the US, in Aotearoa, the psychic and semiotic dynamics of whiteness manifest along the lines of injustice in relationship to housing, employment, the criminal justice system, and education. What de Saxe insightfully reveals is how *Pākehā* not only attempt to obfuscate the reality of their privilege and power (through color-evasion, neoliberal logics, the myth of meritocracy, and the myth of a bicultural nation), but how they continue to denigrate Māori people in various ways (through epistemic exploitation, framing them as a "deficient people," through microaggressions, tokenization, cultural erasure, inculcation and superimposition of white master narratives, blaming them for being "too sensitive" or "too defensive"). What does this say about whiteness within the Aotearoa context? It says to me that white hegemonic dispossession of Māori people continues to exist in multiple and pervasive ways and that whiteness continues to find ways of exercising its oppressive logics while denying the existence of actual oppressors. Therefore, whiteness must be named and resisted, as de Saxe powerfully does throughout her text. It is white people who ought to do the lion's share of the work.

Like de Saxe, I don't see classroom spaces as separate from the larger societal spaces that we inhabit. When students enter my classroom spaces, they don't enter as abstract Cartesian selves, but as embodied selves, having been thrown into the dynamics of history and shaped by heteronomous networks of power and webs of significance. I make a point of explaining to my students that our classroom space is a microcosm of the larger society within which we live. In this way, they are not seduced by the myth that academic spaces/institutions are somehow "sacred" or "pristine." And when whiteness is the topic of critical discussion, I especially encourage my white students to prepare to remove the masks that have for so long concealed their racism, their white power and privilege, and their complicity with racial injustice. de Saxe's pedagogical experience in teaching about whiteness within a university setting in Aotearoa functions as an important exemplar for white teachers who have dared to tackle the topic. White teachers who attempt to critically tarry with whiteness, especially their own whiteness, engage in a process that is by no means easy. As argued earlier, whiteness is not a conceptual puzzle. A puzzle is a task that we (the puzzle solvers) will tackle. We complete puzzles in a number of finite moves, and then we're done. Whiteness is like a many-headed Hydra; it can survive and recenter itself despite efforts to name it, to mark it, to call it out, to dismantle it, to solve it.

White teachers who undertake the project of challenging whiteness within the context of a classroom, face a specific challenge. *They are also the problem.* I say this as white teachers were white long before they became teachers, and they bring their whiteness with them. In my classrooms, I also denounce and critique sexism, but this doesn't mean that I no longer possess the subtleties of the pornographic gaze or am impacted by an imaginary that has been shaped by the historical weight of sexism. de Saxe recognizes that teaching about race and whiteness is a life-long process of learning. The process of critically dismantling and disrupting sexism is also a life-long process.

de Saxe shares her awareness of the ways in which white students run for cover as whiteness is thematized, as they push back against forms of awareness that result in cognitive dissonance. After all, if they are *Pākehā* New Zealanders, they are being asked to explore racial and racist aspects of themselves that they would rather refuse to acknowledge. Overwise that acknowledgement will (or certainly ought to) result in carrying the weight of the harms that they perpetuate from a system that privileges them and oppressively impacts the existence of Māori people. The same applies to white people in the US. They refuse to face their whiteness; they maintain their sense of "innocence" partly through being misled by a neoliberal ontology that supports the myth of meritocracy. To be white within a white supremacist polity is not to exist as a discrete entity, but to be part of a racist past and present that constitutes (not determines) who you are. White people "are, in effect," as James Baldwin (1962/1995) writes, "still trapped in a history which they do not understand; and until they understand it, they cannot be released from it" (p. 8). Indeed, I have known and know white people who teach about race and whiteness and yet fail to recognize the insidiousness of their toxic whiteness, where they squirm (or become outright defiant, red in the face) when they are encouraged to examine further and to explore the possibility that they are by no means free from the institutional, discursive, and psychically opaque sutures of whiteness. In this text, de Saxe critically addresses how she is also aware of unintentionally reproducing the very content that she is working to resist and destabilize. In short, de Saxe is unafraid to name her own vulnerability as she works to undermine the structures of whiteness.

Pedagogically, de Saxe argues that we should create spaces within the classroom where students are able to exercise what she calls unconditional freedom to question. Within universities that have been historically governed by whiteness (where most teachers are white, where the historic figures studied are white, and where the curriculum is white), epistemologies or ways of knowing (and what is known) are also governed by whiteness. Questions that challenge the status quo of whiteness are suppressed *ab initio*. There is nothing magical about this process. It results from what de Saxe refers to as the pipeline of education that has been constructed long ago within societies and polities denominated by white narrative frames that are epistemically dominant and exclusionary with respect to counter-white narratives. After all, this is how whiteness places under erasure counter-memories, ones that contest white canonic memory. Whether in the US, Aotearoa, Canada, or Australia, places where whiteness is systemic, there is an effort to control what is remembered and thereby conceal the reality of the historical conditions that undergird extant forms of racist otherization, discrimination, marginalization, and violence. In the US, the banning of books, the proliferation of lies and disinformation, political and legislative attacks on diversity, equity and inclusion (DEI), and the demonization of Critical Race Theory (indeed, the weaponization of critical thinking itself), are just some of the ways in which the unconditional freedom to question and to think *otherwise* is under attack and being driven primarily by white people who nostalgically desire to Make American Great Again (MAGA).

But what is to be done? I ask this while being under no illusion that there is a quick fix algorithm for dealing with whiteness. Facing educational regimes (and polities) that maintain and reinforce whiteness, de Saxe deploys a very powerful image of the *dangerous citizen*. The use of citizen has both intramural and extramural implications. The dangerous citizen, for de Saxe, is one who resists (takes a stand against) education as a form of social control. To be a dangerous citizen is to be a troublemaker, a gadfly in the face of an educational system and a society designed to maintain lockstep conformity. To be white and to strive to embody the praxis of a dangerous citizen means taking every opportunity to disrupt whiteness, to mark it and render it visible. As Richard Dyer (1997) writes, "Whiteness needs to be made strange" (p.10). For whiteness to be made strange requires white people to exercise a form of self-reflexive agency. In this way, the normative status of whiteness is challenged, one unveils its status as socially constructed, as something masquerading as "ahistorical." This is consistent with what de Saxe sees as debunking a common sense understanding of the world. Whiteness frames the world through a racist episteme that masks the real injustice and violence committed against minoritized Black people, Indigenous people, and People of Color. Common sense, within this context, is a form of epistemic complacency that signals, "Look away. All is as it should be." Within the taken-for-granted world of whiteness, I encourage my white students that their clarion call should be: "*Look, a white!*" That form of interpellation or hailing says that something has gone terribly wrong. And like de Saxe does with respect to Māori traditional knowledge, in my courses on whiteness I epistemologically infuse those pedagogic spaces with the critical voices and testimonies of Black people who have always already known that things have long gone terribly wrong. And my work is not in vain.

I am encouraged when white students share with me that after taking my course they find it hard not to see whiteness in their daily lives. Of course, this experience is discomforting. They must now face the truth that they were mistaken not only about how the world is constructed through white power and privilege, but how they have only begun to personally come to terms with the rabbit hole of whiteness. That pedagogical realization is dangerous precisely because it poses a deep threat to the normatively white status quo, which aims to remain absolute and unquestioned and thereby anti-democratic. Conceived in this way, critical pedagogy poses a real threat to the white epistemic order of things. This is where de Saxe's emphasis on learning to unlearn is so incredibly important, which she links to self-reflexivity, and educating for critical consciousness, and critical theory.

The process of learning to unlearn is a species of kenosis, which is linked to the process of metanoia—a radical mode of turning, of changing, of reorientation. This reorientation involves a form of praxis that encourages a constant effort to de-center whiteness. de Saxe introduces a co-conspiratorial approach that helps to rethink the static identity implied in the concept of the white ally. Etymologically, the term ally means "to bind to." This "binding" can easily function as a form of "being-with," as in "stuck to" as a weight, a burden or a hindrance. In this way, white people give the appearance of anti-racist praxis when in fact it functions as a form of political slumming with a sense of white noblesse oblige. To co-conspire suggests that white people have skin in the game (and they do quite literally). The term implies a deep political and existential commitment on the part of white people to undo the terror of whiteness. It is, as de Saxe notes, a process of constant unsettling or what I call a process of constant white un-suturing. In the end, working *with* BIPOC is the aim of the co-conspiratorial frame. Read radically, it is a process of *breathing* together (given the root meaning of the word conspire) and a collective fidelity to suffer together until the Racial Contract is torn asunder.

Jennifer de Saxe's *Untangling Whiteness: Education, Resistance, and Transformation* is a testimony to her agency, epistemic humility, and transformative hope for what is yet to come. It is conceptually capacious and radically transformative in its understanding, like that of bell hooks, that education is a practice of freedom. In times like these in a world where critical thought is under siege, de Saxe's text is essential.

References

Apple, M. W. (1991). Foreword. In J. L. Kincheloe, S. R. Steinberg, N. M. Rodriguez, & R. E. Chennault (Eds.) *White reign: Deploying whiteness in America.* St. Martin's Press.

Baldwin, J. (1962/1995). *The fire next time.* Modern Library.

Du Bois, W. E. B. (1995). The souls of white folk. In D. L. Lewis (Ed.) *W. E. B. Du Bois: A reader.* Henry Holt.

Dyer, R. (1997). *White.* Routledge.

Freire, P. (2005). *Pedagogy of the oppressed,* 30th Anniversary Edition. Continuum International Publishing Company.

Memmi, A. (2000). *Racism,* Translation with Introduction by Steve Martinot. University of Minnesota Press.

Mills, C. W. (1997). *The racial contract.* Cornell University Press.

Preface

Universities are on the front lines of challenging racial domination and expanding global white supremacy. Because of this, higher education is often targeted for reinforcing 'woke' politics, which, although may challenge race and whiteness from within, tend to have a more difficult time engaging the same level of resistance outside of academia. This is prominent through the banning of books in many countries, the recent US Supreme Court case striking down affirmative action policies for colleges and universities, attacks on the teaching of critical theories of race, and gender, as well as the underfunding and undermining of university education; particularly within the humanities and social sciences. In fact, so much of the way university teaching and learning is conceptualised (at least in my current university) is that learning is content-driven rather than rooted in nuance, critical thinking and active engagement.

'Successful' education (teaching and learning) is often framed and conceptualised through assessment, mastery, and skills that are seen as a necessity in contributing to the global economy. Over the last few decades, the framing of a declining humanities education, as well as an undermining of social science learning as 'the coddling' of the university student (Applebaum, 2021), has co-opted the narrative of a tertiary education that has the potential to interrupt and challenge global inequalities, white supremacy, and unregulated capitalism (Connell, 2007). Education is framed as a competition, whereby standardisation and individualism not only drive the teaching and learning process, but also the way 'success' is socially constructed so that capitalism and whiteness are seen as the norm for achievement and are too often unchecked and normalised. University education further emphasises upward mobility, competition, and the preservation of the status quo. These goals reinforce the seemingly neutral characteristics of individualism and standardisation, framing them as inherently part of the education process, as opposed to something that must be questioned and challenged.

The insidious nature that propels the structural, racial, and institutional oppressions found within both education and society should not be understated. Arguably, this narrative has been so skillfully crafted that both students and professors internalise their own feelings of inferiority, individual failure, and self-defeat (Freire, 1974; Memmi, 1965). Within such a bleak picture of university education, a fatalistic attitude regarding its future would assume the position as the lowest common denominator. However, there are still opportunities for transformation, resistance, and change. Tensions and contradictions need to be teased out, and imagination must be reconceptualised to drive and substantiate change.

All of these challenges sit against a backdrop of a polarised society that can both inadvertently and consciously uphold whiteness, racism, gender discrimination, class, homophobia, transphobia, ableism, and nationalism, (among others). These tensions result in members of society moving further away from, rather than having meaningful conversations around such topics. Thus, as an educatore who teaches about race and white supremacy, I am in a unique and privileged position to reinforce the interconnectivity between what I teach and learn in my university community and its connection to societal change. The two are inextricably linked and mutually inclusive.

Globally, discussions surrounding how to interrupt ongoing histories and practices of institutional and structural racism have become increasingly urgent. Over the past decade, social movements like Black Lives Matter and Free Palestine have dramatically demonstrated the need to find ways to connect on-the-ground community activism with teaching, learning, and transforming society. It is not enough to merely state that one is engaging in anti-racist teaching and learning that matters. Simply taking a 'diversity training' or ticking off a checklist of completed a course on 'racism' is reductionist and simplistic. It is imperative to move beyond the one-dimensional teaching and learning that sees racism and white supremacy in simple binaries of 'racist/not-racist,' as this quickly shuts down meaningful and nuanced understandings of terminology that, if not teased apart, keep them at a distance, resulting in an abdication of responsibility of being complicit in systems that perpetuate and reinforce discrimination, marginalisation, and dehumanisation. Everyone is implicated and is part of a system that upholds and sustains a web of whiteness.

While there are many academics around the world who teach within these concepts and topics, throughout this book, I emphasise the importance of the relationship between a nuanced engagement with critical theories of race and whiteness, the ongoing development of students' and professors' racial consciousness, and the potentialities for societal change and transformation. These learnings require so much more than pedagogical interventions, as the need to complicate students' and ones' various relationships to racial structures is intimately connected to how making sense of, and unpacking the theoretical content and how it might aid in movements of resistance. It is imperative to understand the privileged position one is in as an academic, noting that the students one teaches can disrupt the cycle of avoidance and denial in their respective communities. I am fortunate to teach and learn with students who are instrumental and motivated to challenge the individual, structural, and institutional reproduction of racism, whiteness, and white supremacy. I work to connect with my students in ways that reinforce how, together, we can learn in spaces that are undergirded with collectively and solidarity; some of the most important features of education, resistance, and transformation. However, I also understand that learning critical theories of race and white supremacy is a life-long process that does not begin and end with one course or workshop. It is ongoing and should be part of who I am with my students, as well as how I live my life, both inside and outside of the university classroom.

With the prominence of workshops, trainings, and anti-racist books popping up over the past decade or so, it may seem overwhelming as to what it really means to engage in deliberate and meaningful learning that challenges (in multiple ways) the many facets of whiteness, racism, and white supremacy. This purposeful learning is intimately connected with how one makes sense of and unpacks critical theories of race and whiteness, as they are mutually inclusive and intimately intertwined; both theoretically and in practice. However, it can be reductionist and simplistic if there isn't substantive attention paid to the various relationships and experiences that one has with racial structures and institutions. Without nuance, honesty and care, there is a slippery slope between challenging racial domination, taking ownership of past and present behaviours, and falling into a trap of white tears and expressions of unhealthy guilt about ones' racism and whiteness. Not surprisingly, there are many layers when working to fully understand what it means to 'do the work' whilst aiming to undermine politics, structures, and practices that reproduce racial domination and white supremacy (in its many forms).

What does it mean when someone is told to 'do the work,' or that one says they are engaging in anti-racist teaching and learning? These phrases are some of many that have become part of the social justice and anti-racist parlance over the last few years. I am not arguing that one shouldn't 'do the work' or commit to anti-racism when on the road towards developing racial consciousness, awareness, and the potentialities for societal change. However, when phrases like these sit within nebulous terrain, they can be misinterpreted as an activity that can be started and completed with expediency and detachment. If navigating anti-racist and social justice activism become reduced to one course, a check- list, or even a one-off activity, it can fall into a space of being performative in that it recentres whiteness whilst aiming to dismantle it.

The inspiration and motivation for writing this book are based on a third-year sociology course I teach at my current university in Aotearoa, New Zealand. The course is titled, *Complicating Resistance; Sociology and Transformation.* I have taught this course for four years, and it continues to be my favourite. The content of the course pushes beyond a cursory learning of race and white supremacy. It requires a commitment to sit with the cognitive dissonance (what one has always known to be true is questioned, thus thought confusion) that challenges hegemonic thinking and understandings of racial domination and ideologies of whiteness. I write this book with the same philosophy that I teach the course. Through a deep and multi-faceted interrogation of the many facets of racism and whiteness, this book untangles critical theories of race, whiteness and resistance in an accessible and dialogical manner. This book also situates whiteness in Aotearoa, New Zealand, demonstrating the importance of context and geographic location when working to undermine and interrogate it. As a theoretical provocation of existing scholarship on race and whiteness, this book is underpinned by educating for critical consciousness and self-reflexivity, both of which involve ways that one might interpret the world differently when working to transform it.

I also write this book knowing how busy educators are. Teachers are always trying to read new books, articles, and other mediums that provide opportunities to add to the variety of pedagogies of disruption and critical theory that speak to a range of students, asking them to think about the world in a new way. For this reason, each chapter focuses on a specific concept, theory, or framework. The final chapter is a description of my *Complicating Resistance* course, which hopefully provides readers just one example of how, and in what capacity, the content in the book can be brought into the tenuous and tense university space. I have woven together the theories, ideas, concepts, and scholars that I share with my students when I teach the course on resistance and transformation. The scholars I draw from have all been instrumental in how I understand my own role in upholding whiteness whilst simultaneously working and teaching about interrupting and challenging it at the individual, institutional, and societal level. I am continuously reflecting on this at the cognitive, emotional, intellectual, and practical level. Thus, I engage with, and mirror what I ask of my students and the readers of this book.

This book is written for anyone interested in taking a deeper dive into the teaching and learning of critical theories of race and whiteness. This book does not engage in a debate about whether or not racism exists, or that we live in a society that prioritises and protects whiteness, or that universities reproduce and uphold individual and structural racism and marginalisation. Instead, this book begins with the premise that all of these things are true, and that in order to work towards undermining and interrupting them, there must be an understanding of ones' relationship to the interconnecting systems and practices that uphold these things and keep them true. This book also sees the teaching and learning of race and whiteness not as concepts and theories to define, but rather as ideas, that, although are theoretically grounded and conceptualised, manifest in ways that have real-life ramifications and consequences, individually and structurally. Thus, this book asks, what potentialities may arise if one teases apart *how* these theories manifest, what ones' relationship to them is, and what might happen when marrying these learnings with critical self-reflexivity and educating for critical consciousness? In other words, how can one do this, *and* do that, *and* hold them altogether so that change and transformation can be more than just a utopian ideal? After many years of teaching students in this way, I have seen them do just this. I hope this book brings more people and communities into this orbit.

Although this book is a theoretical provocation on existing theories of race and whiteness, I aim to present and work through these theories in two ways: First, I unpack and discuss each theory so that readers may understand them as part of a framework in which to analyse and make sense of something. For example, in chapter two, I engage the term *intersectionality* as it includes various ways to understand power, diverse forms of marginalisation, and multiple forms of oppression. These ideas come together in a theoretical or conceptual framework as a means by which to step back and analyse a situation, experience, etc, recognising that there are many factors that help to make sense and unpack something. An intersectional framework takes nothing for granted, as individual and societal oppressions are not a one-off but are, in fact, part of a larger system rooted in power and ideologies of race, whiteness, sexism, heteronormativity, etc.

Second, I hope for readers to understand that the critical theories I draw on and analyse can also be deployed as tools of resistance. Understanding and working to engage intersectionality as a tool can be useful when thinking about how to challenge something that does not embody the essence of what it means to be intersectional. One can think of a tool like a pointer finger, in that it focuses specifically on something that must be questioned, ultimately aiming towards unsettling and transforming it. I see the potentiality of looking to intersectionality as a tool of resistance, as it directly confronts and calls out inequitable or oppressive systems, policies, agendas, etc, with the goal of challenging and changing them. In other words, intersectionality as a framework provides a nuanced manner to step back and analyse something, whereas intersectionality as a tool, provides the opportunity to step back in and directly challenge something that is not demonstrating intersectionality in philosophy or practice.

I have organised the six chapters in this book the same way that I teach the first six lectures of the course. The first chapter foregrounds and situates the readers in a space that prepares them for the active and purposeful engagement that is intimately part of the process of learning and unlearning. I discuss many concepts that connect with how I deploy educating for critical consciousness and critical self-reflexivity, which is what I hope the readers can do alongside the learning of the critical theories in chapters two through five. I reinforce the importance of locating ones' racialised selves directly within the learning process, as without doing so, the content can sit at a comfortable distance so as to keep oneself out of the discussion. Chapters two through five are theoretical provocations on critical theories of race and whiteness. Throughout these chapters, I situate their conceptual and theoretical meanings and how they manifest in both the United States and Aotearoa, New Zealand. I do this to demonstrate the context and concept-specific nature of terminology that is understood differently around the globe. I end the book with a description of my sociology course, *Complicating Resistance,* which includes a discussion of the racial autobiography assignment, a pivotal assessment that is at the heart of the class as well as at the heart of this book.

My goal in writing this book is for readers to zoom out, take nothing for granted, and hold onto multiple ideas simultaneously. For white readers, the purposes and lenses will be quite different than for readers who are Black, Indigenous and People of Colour (BIPOC). I draw from scholars of critical race theory, critical whiteness studies, critical feminist and queer theories, as well as critical educators, sociologists, and philosophers. Although some of the concepts might be discussed independently of one another, they rely and build on each other to uphold the many ways that a matrix or a web of whiteness is maintained and sustained, particularly within the university. Thus, the discussion and analyses are quite interdisciplinary and multi-dimensional.

In 2023, I was asked to speak about the *Complicating Resistance* course I teach for a podcast series [1]that is run through my current university. Sharing and talking about my teaching, particularly about a course like the one I discuss in chapter six, is an uncomfortable exercise for me. On the one hand, I believe it is important to speak about my teaching pedagogy and how I believe my students (and myself) have genuinely learned and grown as critically-minded beings throughout the course. However, I often resist talking about the way I teach, as I see it as such a personal and communal experience I have with my students and tutors, that I worry sharing about the intricacies of the course might undermine the work and trust I build with all those involved. Thus, when asked to discuss the course, I saw it as an opportunity to include former students who took it and tutored with me over the last few years. It seemed the perfect opportunity to convey the essence of the teaching, learning and collective sharing that undergirds what it means to see education as the practice of freedom and critical theory being liberatory. In a way, it provided the three of us an opportunity to embody what hooks'(1994) describes as engaged pedagogy and self-actualisation. During the podcast, the three of us discussed the multiple ways we are racialised, the experiences (or lack thereof) in taking courses that centre race and whiteness, as well as the transformative power of education that has the potential to challenge the many ways whiteness and racial domination permeate both the university spaces and society. I end this preface with a quote from bell hooks about engaged pedagogy:

> To teach in varied communities not only our paradigms must shift but also the way we think, write, speak. The engaged voice must never be fixed and absolute but always changing, always evolving in dialogue with a world beyond itself (1994, p.11).

---

[1] The Rebellious Minds podcast runs a series on radical and engaging teaching and learning of topics that are challenging and potentially controversial.

PART 1

Chapter one discusses educating for critical consciousness and critical self-reflexivity, both of which engage the active learning process needed when working to interrupt, undermine, and challenge whiteness and racial domination within education and society. This first chapter situates the readers in a space that asks them to consider their racialised selves through standpoint and positionality, noting how the entirety of ones' various identities and experiences are connected with and through the content of the book, albeit in different ways. Chapter two unpacks critical theory and intersectionality, both of which speak to the liberatory potential of concepts and ideas that centre ones' lived experiences and their connection to liberation. Specifically, chapter two discusses how intersectionality (and its connection to critical theory) may be deployed as a framework in which to analyse education and society. Through three particular tenets, or lenses, I further demonstrate how critical theory and intersectionality have the potential to expose taken-for-granted policies, philosophies, and ones' diverse experiences in the world, particularly as they relate to university education. Chapter two deploys intersectionality and critical theory as a framework and lens in order to zoom out, make sense of, and think differently about the many ways that the university upholds and maintains whiteness and racial domination. Accordingly, part one of the book foregrounds the readers with the necessary frameworks, language, and ideas that prepare them to actively read the chapters in part two. Additionally, the sequence of the content within part one is scaffolded so that readers can move directly into the subsequent chapters in part two, understanding the nuance and multi-faceted discussions and analyses that are needed to fully immerse themselves in the book in its entirety.

Chapter 1

Critical Self-reflexivity and Educating for Critical Consciousness

Introduction

There must be some cognitive breakthrough on a level of 'common sense,' a development of critical awareness of power and one's social location within that power, *and* experiencing a felt sense of compassion and accountability, *and* are provided with an alternative ideological, conceptual, and interpretive frameworks which give language and structure to ones' cognitive and emotional shifts. Only through this interconnectivity can praxis[1] and transformation actualise (Perry & Shotwelll, 2009).

What does it mean to think in a critically self-reflexive way? How does one take part in the practice of critical self-reflexivity? In what ways does critical self-reflexivity intersect with educating for critical consciousness, learning critical theory and being action-oriented? These are questions this chapter develops. Every reader comes to this book with their own racialised experiences and perspectives. When I use the terms racialised or racialisation, I refer to how one is taught, treated, understands, experiences, and 'does' race. Everyone is socialised in their relationship with race, as well as how they make sense of and 'act' as racialised beings. Being racialised reinforces biases and stereotypes that are either confirmed or denied in interpersonal relationships, observations, and experiences. These are not accidental processes. Racialisation relies on the meanings of ideas and concepts such as race and whiteness, as well as their agreed upon (or hegemonically agreed upon) understandings within society. For example, when a white person experiences their identity that is 'racialised as white,' this means that opaqueness, or 'normalcy' of identifying as white deems one as not having race. Within this perspective, ones' understanding

---

[1] Throughout this book, *praxis* is defined as the learning of theory and the practical application or humanising of theory.

and experience whilst living as white is the default status, in that they do not often have to think about it, as within segregated communities, everyone they might know, engage, or live with might be white. In other words, ones' white identity and being racialised and living as white denotes the idea or concept of race as existing in juxtaposition to Black, Indigenous and People of Colour (BIPOC). Whiteness only becomes exposed when a person of colour is around. Otherwise, whiteness is deemed invisible. Being racialised as white absolves whites from thinking about their whiteness or about the meaning of race, as whiteness is not named, it is 'normal,' it is the default. For those who were/are socialised and live as white, they can comfortably stay on course behaving and seeing themselves as raceless and in ways that they have always known, feel comfortable with, and understand. Conversely, by learning what it means to be socialised as white, one can proactively and critically work towards interrogating it, whilst challenging its hegemony and opaqueness.

This chapter begins with this very premise; each person brings their individual experiences of racialisation to the teaching and learning process, as well as how they are operationalised within educational communities. The ways one is racialised and lives are intimately connected with how one understands and thinks about their relationship to critical theories of race and whiteness, as well as how ones chooses to respond and engage with such theory. Additionally, making sense of the racialisation process is inextricably linked to how one learns about this process, as well as the manner in which one chooses to act in response to such teaching and learning. The process of understanding oneself as a racialised being, how this interpretation of oneself connects with an engagement of critical theories of race, and what sort of action one takes when working towards educating for critical consciousness and critical self-reflexivity is the essence of this chapter. I draw on a variety of ideas to make sense of, learn, and consider these processes. Additionally, I discuss some of the ways one might think about their relationship to educating for critical consciousness and critical self-reflexivity. These ideas and their connection to institutional and societal resistance and transformation are intimately connected to the active learning and thinking that is inherently part of the ethos and purpose of this book.

I begin the first section of this chapter by discussing Paulo Freire and his life's work of educating for critical consciousness. Drawing on Freire's philosophy of liberatory education and coming to critical consciousness, I demonstrate the importance of conceptualising education as dialogical, dialectical, and emancipatory. Engaging education in these ways requires a commitment to communal and collective learning and unlearning. Freire's philosophy seeks to understand oneself as an unfinished being, noting how ones' awareness of race is that it is a process of socialisation that is not static or fixed, but rather, is malleable and amenable to change. I further develop the philosophical ideas of education as liberation by drawing on Gert Biesta and Maxine Greene, as they both echo Freire's call for educating for critical consciousness.

The second section of this chapter brings together the various dimensions that speak to the practice of critical self-reflexivity; specifically focusing on feminist and racial standpoint theories and positionality. Both theories and ways of critically reflecting provide an opportunity to understand gendered and racialised selves. Critical self-reflexivity is not something that is often encouraged or developed in academia, thus there is a risk that when engaging in such a process, (even with the best of intentions) one may unintentionally undermine it and become self-referential. Thus, I discuss some of the potential roadblocks that might prevent someone from fully committing themself to the process of working towards critical self-reflexivity and how one can come to understand themself as racialised and socialised beings. Within the context of being racialised as white, I present and discuss the *good white* paradox (Applebaum, 2021) and being a *white problem,* (Yancy, 2105) both of which critique centring whiteness as opposed to overtly challenging and critiquing it.

Finally, I underscore the importance of committing to the multi-faceted nature of learning that activates spaces to educate for critical consciousness whilst working towards developing practices for ongoing critical self-reflexivity. Learning and understanding critical theory, unsettling ones' racialised selves, and aiming towards action and reflection are not linear nor are they easy processes to embody and embrace. Thus, I discuss how to engage the philosophies and practices of cultural humility, generosity, and staying in the conversation; all of which provide some of the tools and dispositions needed to embrace the internal gymnastics that often accompany such learning, unlearning, and reflecting.

Educating for Critical Consciousness

True dialogue cannot exist unless the dialoguers engage in critical thinking-thinking which discerns an indivisible solidarity between the world and the people and admits of no dichotomy between them-thinking which perceives reality as process as transformation, rather than as a static entity- thinking which does not separate itself from action, but consistently immerses itself in temporality without fear of the risks involved (Freire, 1970, p.92).

As the essence of this book connects learning, unlearning, and seeing education as a lifelong process, I draw on and honour the work of radical educator and pedagogue Paulo Freire. Freire (1970, 1974, 1998) understands education and society as inextricably linked, and connected to liberation and freedom. There must be a proactive engagement with an honest and open mind and heart when aiming towards rethinking the manner in which to challenge white supremacy and racial domination. Freire argues that the process of educating for critical consciousness is directly connected to being with and within the world. It intersects the learning of critical theory, critical self-reflexivity, and works towards action-oriented processes that challenge multiple forms of oppression. Educating for critical consciousness requires a commitment to understanding and challenging the many ways that whiteness, power and racial domination intersect. It further embodies the process of unlearning and relearning, as they are dialogical and have the potential to reshape how one lives their life, thus equipping them to move about the world differently.

Freire further sees educating for critical consciousness as being *in* and *with* one's reality, and that within every understanding, sooner or later, an action corresponds. Freire states, "conscientization is the important initial stage of transformation-that historical moment when one begins to think critically about the self and identity in relation to one's political circumstances" (1974, 47). In other words, one must examine the individual and/or collective forms of oppression as the starting points, (one's reality) from which to then move forward to combat and free oneself from such oppression through critical action and intervention (de Saxe, 2021). Embodying the tenets of educating for critical consciousness, Freire seeks to change minds, and senses of being. By thinking about the process of developing a critical awareness of ones' social reality through reflection and action, therein lies the possibility of understanding action as fundamental because it has the potential to change reality. Within this context, *critical self-reflexivity* becomes an internal project that has the potential to collectively challenge the many dimensions of whiteness, ultimately aiming towards societal transformation. When engaging in the practice of self-reflexivity, a process is activated to develop a critical awareness of social reality through reflection and action. Action is fundamental because it is a means of changing reality.

Freire (1970) further argues for the importance of locating critical consciousness as a set of linguistic tools as they have a foundation within the social and political visions of various revolutionary critical race thinkers. Linguistic tools help to name problems which were previously un-named, and to develop a moving language for talking about them in the context of the wider university and society (de Saxe and Trotter-Simons, 2021). Critically, this language must then shape the direction of subsequent action (Lorde, 1984, pp. 36-37). Au (2012) furthers this notion of a dialectic of consciousness which recognises that everyone is simultaneous with and within the world. It is what intertwines and connects the world and community both inside and outside of educational communities. One comes to know things vis-à-vis their inseparable relationships with the totality of their environments. The dialectics of consciousness underscores how educational institutions and classrooms are simply a microcosm of society. The interconnectedness between the two spaces is fluid in nature, evolving, and moving together. Each person is in the classroom and in the world simultaneously.

One way to consider liberatory and emancipatory changes within the larger community is to engage dialectically and democratically in educational institutions. Biesta, (2006) calls on both educators and students to question and consider what it means to be human. He understands this question as the basic tenet for looking at education as something that should be responsible for fostering and exploring the uniqueness of each individual. Biesta argues that many educational institutions do not allow for difference or plurality. Instead, he notes that educational communities (at all levels) often push students to subscribe to the only community the school knows: *the rational community*. Through a rational community, Biesta iterates that the function of many educational institutions is not to teach students how to speak their own languages, with their specific ideas, understandings, and perspectives, but rather they serve as places where students will learn the 'only way to speak' (i.e.; dominant and hegemonic language and epistemologies). Thus, educational institutions, whilst teaching only one way to communicate, are simultaneously delegitimising any other way of speaking. Differences or plurality are often regarded as dangerous and as something that would disrupt the very rational community that education re-creates and fosters year after year. It is imperative to move towards learning communities that embrace and acknowledge difference, subjugated knowledges, and plurality. Only within such spaces can education be actualised as liberatory, healing, and democratic (Biesta, 2006).

To further a conceptualisation of education as empowering and transformative, I draw on Greene (1998) and her philosophy of reconceptualising human freedom and liberatory education. Greene considers the following questions:

> How much does the possibility of freedom depend on critical reflectiveness, on self-understanding, on insight into the world? How much does it depend on being with others in a caring relationship? How much depends on actually coming together with unknown others in a similar predicament, in an "existential project," reaching toward what is not yet? (Greene, p.79)

Greene argues that freedom can only be actualised in public spaces where individuals can be in the presence of others, and where thoughtful discussions and potential action and resistance may take place. Greene understands such spaces as communities where people can challenge, seek alternatives, and come together in solidarity, ultimately aiming for truly empowering and liberatory education. Most important, Greene believes that people are deprived of their true freedom when there is no public space to proactively participate with others. She underscores the importance of opening up spaces so that students and educators can remake and reimagine democratic communities. Greene focuses on bringing in new voices, new perspectives, and working towards alternative ways of teaching and learning, ultimately leading to what may be actualised as transformative and liberatory education. Such a way of being with and within the world cultivates diverse perspectives, and creates spaces for shared empowerment, imagination, and freedom.

It is this active (often discomforted) philosophy and engagement within university and classroom spaces that I argue has the potential to reframe how to teach, learn, and move about the world. Apple and Buras (2006) speak to this point by stating, "consciousness of relations of subordination and domination is the first step in moving towards the critical sensibility needed to build counterhegemonic movements in education and elsewhere" (p. 282). There is an intimate interconnectivity between education and the cognitive dissonance that occurs when engaging with material that challenges a 'common sense' understanding of the world. It is precisely through a domain of educating for critical consciousness and critical self-reflexivity that has the potential to interweave critical theory and resistance in ways that have the potential to interrupt and challenge whiteness and racial domination. However, attention must first be paid to how ones' racialised and gendered selves are interconnected with the processes of learning and unlearning; i.e.: critical self-reflexivity. The following section discusses feminist and racial standpoint theories, both of which demonstrate and reinforce the ways that ones' gendered and racial identities are socially constructed, yet are also very real when connecting with how one thinks, interprets, and behaves within the world.

Feminist and Racial Standpoint Theory

Developing the idea of feminist standpoint theory, Code (1991) argues for the importance of drawing on feminist standpoint when conducting academic research. She underscores how knowledge is both objective and subjective, and that the gender of the knower is epistemologically significant. Code states, "facts may mean different things to different people, affect some people profoundly, and others not at all: hence they are both subjective and objective" (p.45). Significantly, she understands the paradox of autonomy in feminist thought; "The autonomy obsession of androcentric thinking endorses a stark conception of individualism that overemphasises self-realisation and self-reliance. I have argued against the supremacy of these values in favor of 'second personhood' and mutuality" (p.275). Code further recognises the struggle for autonomy which many women strive toward in their pursuit of feminist theory and action. Accordingly, "feminists have urged women to strive for autonomy, both as freedom *from* patriarchal oppression and as freedom *to* realise their capacities and aspirations" (Code, p.73). However, when women become autonomous, they lose a part of themselves that has the potential to help in their pursuit of personal knowledge, understanding, and a communal basis of moral and mental activity. Most important, autonomy, individuality, and competition are the antithesis of engaging with feminism as a collective and collaborative movement.

Code recognises this paradox through her critique of the concept essentialising. She reinforces the damage such a generalisation can have on feminist epistemology. By searching to find common voice and experiences, differences in race, class, gender, sexuality, (among others) are neglected. Code engages the importance of feminist thought and feminist critical theory uniting and moving forward as women, however, there must be wariness of speaking of and for all women. "Feminists need to demonstrate the reality of social injustices and practices, and to work as hard for change in larger social structures and institutions as for change in the 'personal' areas of womens' lives" (p.320). Code's interpretation privileges women to stand together but recognises the need to define individuality, whilst avoiding tokenising experiences within marginalised groups. Just as a white women's experience would not be universalised to all white women, nor should Black or Women of

Colour's experience be reduced to a singular interpretation. Thus, feminist standpoint requires close attention be paid to race, (both self-identified and/or ascribed) and its connection to positionality.

Racial Standpoint and Positionality

Racial standpoint, building on similar characteristics to that of the feminist standpoint, exists in opposition to dominant cultural systems such as whiteness as an ideology, white supremacy, and hegemonic epistemologies (Au, 2012; Collins, 2000; Kinefuchi & Orbe, 2008). Such vantage points are a result of one's field of experience (or social location) and are often used to better understand how people come to see and experience the world differently. Racial standpoint is most evident with those who have the most and least power in society as it relates to their race and ethnicity. Thus, white/European, and Black, Indigenous, and People of Colour have different understandings, experiences, and meanings of the world. Individuals who are marginalised or minoritised (self-identified or ascribed) as well as those with a white racial identity (also self-identified or ascribed) are influenced by how they understand their lived realities and the world around them.

I deploy the term minoritised rather than minority, as when used as a verb, the term highlights the often active and oppressive experiences many BIPOC people face and are subjected to. If one is designated as having a minoritised status, they are seen as an 'Other' or the opposite from what is deemed 'normal,' or what is hegemonically understood and conceptualised as white. Additionally, the person who deploys the term minority, speaks from their specific standpoint, usually seeing their perspective as the dominant one, thus denoting someone or a group who is not a member of the dominant group. As I argue that nothing is taken for granted, specifically language, I highlight how terminology is situated and how it is connected to stereotypes, understood, framed, and acted upon within societies. To provide another example of language rephrasing, consider what happens when using the term 'emergent bilingual' rather than 'English language learner.' In countries and societies that prioritise the English language as the dominant language, the meaning of the phrase denotes a change in perspective and interpretation so that by referring to someone as an emergent bilingual, they are described as having an asset rather than a deficit, which is often part of the definition used when identifying and labelling someone as an English language learner.

Social locations also shape peoples' lives (race, class, gender, sexuality, etc.) and have different, often oppositional standings (Collins, 1990). Collins argues, "while common experiences may predispose Black women to develop a distinctive group consciousness, they guarantee neither that such a consciousness will develop among all women nor that it will be articulated as such by the group" (p. 24). Furthermore, racial standpoint refers to more than just social location, experience, or perspective. It encompasses a critical and oppositional understanding of how one's life is shaped by larger social and political forces.

Racial standpoints are dialectic and fundamentally collective. Within this perspective, Collins reinforces the argument that one must be careful of generalising and essentialising:

> No homogenous Black *woman's* standpoint exists. There is no essential or archetypal Black woman whose experiences stand as normal, normative, and thereby authentic. An essentialist understanding of Black woman's standpoint suppresses differences among Black women in search of an elusive group unity (Collins, p.28)

Positionality, on the other hand, refers to proximity (attached or detached) within which people interact and understand the world. Positionality might include opinions, values, beliefs, experiences, etc., as well as how an individual identity and affiliation are positioned and interpreted by others (Kinefuchi & Orbe, 2008). For example, two individuals from the same racial group may acknowledge their shared racial location, but may differ in their positionality and life experiences. These examples further challenge the practice of essentialising, and situate the complexity of race, as well as demonstrate points of divergence and convergence with others.

Another way to interpret standpoint, positionality, and self-reflexivity, is to consider the notion of a *double image*. Drawing from and extending on Dubois' theory known as double consciousness, (1903,1994) Seidl and Hancock, (2011) develop the idea of a double image. Per Seidl and Hancock, a double image provides "white people with insight into the images they project in cross-raced encounters, allowing them to anticipate the ways Black and People of Colour might perceive some of their behaviours, responses, and beliefs and to understand the emotions these might raise" (p. 688-689). Accordingly, this is not an easy practice to engage when working towards naming and challenging whiteness. Seidl and Hancock articulate:

> The very fact that most Whites can move in and out of a double image, depending on the context, denotes the maintenance of their privileged position. Similarly, the fact that such an image is temporary for most

Whites, given their movement in and out of places occupied by People of Color, is neither good nor bad; rather, it is the outcome of our society's structure of oppression and dominance. (p. 695)

Drawing on ones' standpoint and positionality whilst learning critical theories of race and whiteness is vital when seeking to make sense of individual and institutional cultures and structures that uphold and normalise whiteness. Standpoint and positionality overlap and interconnect, providing the necessary connection and reflexivity needed when learning to think differently about the many dimensions of untangling race and whiteness. It is too easy for white people to gloss over the complexities of whiteness, obscuring and/or evading one's implication within the very systems and structures they seek to interrogate and work to dismantle. In fact, taking a deep dive into the nuances that make up the intricacies of whiteness and one's complicity within them (both intentionally and unintentionally) is not only a privilege, but it is also a choice. Part of identifying and being socialised as white is deciding when, how, and if one chooses to take up the work of developing a white racial consciousness (McHugh, 2015). However, to truly commit oneself to this process, white people must come to a point and understanding that in a racist world, white people will always be a problem, and there must be vigilance about white racism and the institutional racism that whites benefit from. Within this perspective, whites must reflect on how learning and action are interconnected. This is not an easy nor a streamlined process. In fact, without awareness of some of the ways whiteness is upheld, sidestepped, centered and recentered, it becomes too easy to fall into a trap that derails even the best of intentions.

'Being a Problem' and the 'Good White'

To reiterate, everyone is a racialised being who brings the totality of themselves and their experiences to the learning process. It is common for uncomfortable feelings to arise, particularly for whites who have been socialised to see themselves as raceless and cultureless. Thus, educating for, and coming to critical consciousness, is a process that requires self-reflexivity, which, for many whites, includes seeing and understanding themselves as the problem. As Applebaum (2021) argues, part of being a white problem is having the privilege to abdicate any responsibility for how society is set up so cleverly and meticulously to cater to white advantages. The world of whiteness with such benefits is that whiteness is the default or that which is deemed 'normal.' The essence of whiteness is that it is too easily seen and experienced as shaping an ordinary lived reality; it is both an orderliness and an ordinariness (Teel, 2015).

As McHugh iterates, "in choosing to challenge and to work to dismantle my whiteness, to be willing to feel this 'strangeness,' I at the same time am experiencing a privilege of being white" (p.150). Herein lies the importance of situating one's social and racial location, as well as activating one's positionality, as they are intimately connected to how one responds and works to untangle the many manifestations of whiteness.

I circle back to the concept or practice of a double image, and the significance of interrogating the 'normalcy' and opaqueness of whiteness. As stated above, whites must work towards developing an identity that includes the various ways they are perceived as white. This process of unsettling whiteness speaks to understanding whiteness as a hermeneutics of the self, in that it is more of an ideological choice than a biological destiny. If whites look to whiteness as a hermeneutics of empathy, they "reserve hope that whiteness may emerge as an authentic worldview . . . white racism is inherently oppressive, but whiteness, seen through the prism of reconstructionism, is multifaceted and undecidable" (Leonardo, 2009, p.127). What potentialities may arise by engaging with an affective understanding for how unlearning whiteness may assist in reconfiguring a hegemonic and ideological interpretation of whiteness (Perry & Shotwell, 2009)? Giving language to affective experiences must coincide with the shift that occurs when challenging ideologies of whiteness.

Further, Applebaum (2021) argues that the *ambiguity* of white supremacy is fundamental in upholding the many dimensions of whiteness. Within a context of ambiguity, whites can sit in a space of uncertainty, which by default, allows for inaction and avoidance. Ambiguity is nebulous enough that it is hard to pin down and explicitly call out. When things are even slightly unclear, they can be excused away or brushed off. Bailey (2015) connects with this idea of ambiguity through a practice called 'white talk.' The intent of white talk is to uphold evasive behaviour when unpacking and working to understand whiteness. Specifically, Bailey states, "white talk is designed, indeed scripted, for the purposes of evading, rejecting, and remaining ignorant about the injustices that flow from whiteness and its attendant privileges" (p.39/40). White talk steers clear of any suggestions that white people's own actions, thoughts, behaviours, etc., may in fact contribute to the perpetuation of racial ignorance. It is also what allows many whites the ability to abdicate responsibility in claiming their racism, as too often white racial enlightenment comes with the othering of whites less 'advanced' in their white racial awareness. Notably, it is easier and more common for individual whites to relinquish responsibility and to see other whites as part of the problem. In fact, Applebaum (2015) pays close attention to where whites believe they fit on the 'hierarchy of enlightenment' when measuring their understanding of whiteness.

> In what might seem like a paradox, white benevolence is an important site to interrogate the type of problem that white complicity is. White benevolence not only comes with implicit requisite demands but might also function to silence those upon whom benevolence is bestowed. Because benevolence is considered 'good,' the one who bestows the benevolence has in effect secured his/her innocence and does not have to questions his/her implication of injustice (p.3).

Oftentimes, what starts out as a proactive and productive step in unsettling and challenging one's relationship with whiteness can quickly recentre it even when not intending to do so. For example, a common and simple phrase and question can put the work back onto someone else, whilst simultaneously turning the focus of the work inward so that it self-congratulatory and something to esteem towards. I provide the following example from Pollock et al., 2009, and their article about preservice teachers and how they work towards activating their understanding of whiteness and its connection to anti-racist teaching and learning. The phrase *What can I do?*, presents an opportunity to tease it apart and see what happens when the focus of the question shifts. Regardless of which word in this question is highlighted, (What can **I** do, **What** can I do, and What **can** I do?), the assumption is that one must individually *do* something specific and/or tangible in order to quickly and effectively dismantle systems, or matrices of whiteness that uphold racial domination and hegemonies of whiteness. They further note that within this space, the person asking the question needs concrete methods or tools, rather than ideas that provide them an opportunity to think differently about whiteness. Further, the phrase emphasises a commitment to individual acts rather than imagining structural change, as well as demanding personal development before societal improvement is even possible (or vice versa in each case). Within this example, the 'good white' needs to see and conceptualise themselves at being at the centre of activating such change. As Yancy (2012) so firmly declares, anti-racist whites can still be white racists. The 'good white' persona can easily derail into a performative act when there is a lack of awareness for how good intentions can spill over into complicit and uncritical behaviour that upholds, rather than works to tear down the stronghold of whiteness.

Significantly, and drawing on critical self-reflexivity and one's awareness of their standpoint and positionality, Leonardo (2009) posits that one can directly confront whiteness in a transformative rather than performative way. Leonardo deploys the term *white reconstructionism*, which creates a space for discourse that works to transform whiteness, and white people, into something other than an oppressive ideology and identity. It aims for a "rearticulated form of whiteness that reclaims its identity for racial justice...Whiteness is a privilege, but whites can use this privilege for purposes of racial justice and therefore contribute to the remaking of whiteness that is not inherently oppressive and false" (p. 124). These critical approaches to rethinking whiteness shift the white racial project from a perspective of dominance to that which is justice-oriented. This mind-shifting that challenges centring whiteness has the potential to directly confront whiteness, as it is undergirded with understanding the significance of educating for critical consciousness and self-reflexivity. To engage the notion of unfinished beings is to recognise the potentialities that might arise when challenging oneself to think differently about living, doing, and being racialised as white. Thus, I move to how one might begin and continue to shift their thinking in ways that reconceptualise or rearticulate whiteness by drawing on the work of a few scholars within critical whiteness studies. This frontloading is an important first step when situating oneself in a space to be fully present in the teaching and learning process.

Rearticulating Whiteness

What might the practice of unsettling and challenging whiteness look like, particularly within the university classroom and community? Drawing on the tenets of educating for critical consciousness and critical self-reflexivity, educators and students have the tools and opportunities to create spaces that can undermine the oppressive power of whiteness. White people have the potential to challenge themselves by radically questioning the workings of white supremacy and breaking an oath of loyalty to whiteness. Whites must consider their roles in upholding whiteness within teaching and learning spaces so as to move about the world differently. How and in what capacity do white people contribute to the interconnected systems of racial domination and oppression? White people must become an integral component of the protestation of institutions and structures that create, perpetuate, and maintain the privileging of whiteness and white domination.

From a teaching and learning perspective, I draw on Haviland, (2008) who engages in a practice called *white educational discourse*. At the practical level, white educational discourse is just one way that whites can insidiously and subversively explain away their complicity in upholding whiteness, i.e., being a problem. This behaviour is further apparent through Gordon's (2022) metaphor of keeping the elephant in the room. Gordon describes upholding the elephant in the room as avoiding a direct conversation of calling out and confronting whiteness. He argues that as a practice, avoiding something that is obviously there takes more effort than it would to discuss it. Gordon notes that through white educational discourse and avoidance, whiteness becomes more present and overt. It seems that the motivation for keeping the elephant in the room is the discomfort, fear, and denial of discussing or exposing it, as in fact, a *presence*. This fear is often connected with what one may learn about themselves. It insulates people from being or feeling implicated in social inequality, valuing social cohesion over challenge, and promoting a noncritical stance when discussing or understanding race, racism, and white supremacy. Within such a situation, emotions (generally of guilt or defensiveness) take over to deflect real issues or to steer conversations toward comfort zones where one can feel safe. White people often dominate many facets of life but tend not to be conscious of this power.

Thus, how might white people understand themselves as a problem, whilst actively untangling and challenging it? Looking at the concept of *third-wave whiteness*, Twine and Gallagher (2008) move beyond thinking about whiteness and its 'exposure, yet invisibility' and towards a reality that challenges the perpetuation of power and privilege, i.e.; naming the elephant in the room. Twine and Gallagher first recognise the interdisciplinary nature of third-wave whiteness (owing a significant debt to feminist scholarship on race), noting that "this diverse scholarship is linked by a common denominator- an examination of how power and oppression are articulated, redefined and reasserted through various political discourses and cultural practices that privilege whiteness even when the prerogatives of the dominant group are contested" (p.7). One of the aims of third-wave whiteness is to decentre the conversation of whiteness that often occurs as a strategy for denial and protection (Solomona et al., 2006) and instead, expose it as a structural and social construct (with real-life ramifications and consequences) with the aim of challenging and unsettling it as opposed to seeing it as 'invisible' or unmarked (McIntosh, 1990). By understanding, naming, and tracking whiteness and how it is constructed socially and historically, therein lies the possibilities of revealing its various operations to challenge and renegotiate its meanings. One of the features that differentiates third-wave whiteness from other scholarship on whiteness is its avoidance of essentialising accounts of whiteness. Instead, third-wave whiteness sees whiteness as a multiplicity of identities that are historically grounded, class-specific, politically manipulated, and gendered social locations that inhabit local custom and national sentiments within the context of the new 'global village' (Twine and Gallagher, 2008). One of the central foci of third-wave whiteness is how one makes sense of the many nuances surrounding the often-tenuous, situational, and relational power that whiteness plays in one's everyday public and private life.

Finally, how might one connect these ideas, theories, and practices within an educational setting? Matias and Mackey's (2016) discuss a *pedagogisation of critical whiteness studies*. Falling in-line with the practice of critical self-reflexivity as it relates to understanding one's complicity with white supremacy, a pedagogy of critical whiteness becomes an active framework which deconstructs the material, physical, emotional, and political power of whiteness. Used in conjunction with other critical theories of race, critical whiteness studies provide a *yin* to the *yang* studies of race. A true commitment to anti-racist teaching and learning cannot be fully actualised by choosing to ignore how the exertions of whiteness create a violent condition for survival. As Yancy (2018) notes, 'as you reap comfort from being white, we suffer for being Black and People of Colour. But your comfort is linked to our pain and suffering' (p. 22).

Although this book engages many theories that ask, seek to understand, and work to make sense of the theoretical and conceptual facets of whiteness and race, it is not a book that provides 'knowledge' in the traditional sense. The knowledge learnt is to gain a better understanding of the many ways that one might be implicated in how whiteness upholds power, systems, and structures of domination and hegemony. How can whites get to a place that assists in activating critical self-reflexivity and educating for critical consciousness at the same time as working to understand critical theories of race and whiteness? This is not an easy task, as it is often easier to learn passively and distance oneself from this cognitive and mental gymnastics. However, by considering the practices of cultural humility and 'staying in the conversation,' therein lies an opportunity to interrupt and challenge whiteness and racial domination.

A Framework of Cultural Humility and Staying in the Conversation[2]

The concept of cultural humility embraces critical self-reflexivity and lifelong learning, institutional accountability, and recognises and challenges power imbalances (Tervalon and Murray-Garcia, 1998). Active and generous learning

---

[2] I draw on Aanerud (2015) and her discussion of a pedagogy of humility in her chapter "Humility and Whiteness: "How Did I Look without Seeing, Hear without Listening?"

and listening are ongoing practices that require one to situate their racial standpoints and positionality *within* conversations around race and whiteness, rather than seeing oneself as separate from these discourses.

A framework of humility may be deployed when engaging learning that asks one to think deeply and purposefully with and about critical theories of race and whiteness. Humility does not mean to humiliate. On the contrary, it serves to inspire clarity and accountability, as it pays attention to what one knows or thinks one knows, and to sit within a space of uncertainty and discomfort. Aaaerud (2105) distinguishes the practice of humility from that of humiliating. She states,

> By humility I am not suggesting self-effacement or something akin to moral virtue, rather I am suggesting a conception of the self as accountable, interconnected, and open to cognitive uncertainty and mystery... humility is an inescapable aspect or condition of an ethical social existence (p. 105).

Further, humility and its connection to strategically, reflexive practice is privileged as the site where one can learn how to turn critical thought into emancipatory action. This entails a type of reflexivity that pays attention to the politics of what one does and does not do at a practical level (Lather, 1991, p.13). It also requires action energised with a type of vigilance that is rooted in self-critique (Foste, 2020). Humility is also about strength, in that one must recognise that knowledge is always limited and that this is not a deficit but a crucial source of information.

Invoking a sense of humility challenges the goal of becoming an 'expert,' (which often arises within the cultural competency discourse) and fosters a willingness to stay within a space of uncertainty. A framework of cultural humility focuses on the ongoing need for accountability, and being aware of the inescapability of the interconnection of all things. Most important, the practice of cultural humility, its connection to uncertainty and contemplative thinking, does not need to result in 'T'ruth and knowledge, in the traditional sense.

Connecting with a framework of humility can also be conceptualised as 'staying in the conversation.' Watson (2018) argues for the importance of creating a classroom environment that welcomes honesty, disagreement, and respect. This is imperative when working to move beyond simplistic notions of understanding whiteness and race. Watson underscores the importance of rapt listening, giving of self, and being fully present when unpacking one's own racial standpoint, positionality, and how one comes to understanding themselves as racialised beings. As difficult emotions and feelings often arise through this practice, I echo Watson's description of creating a 'safe space.' Watson conceptualises a safe space:

> By 'safe,' I don't mean a place where folks won't get offended, or angry, or feel pain. I mean safe enough to feel all of these emotions and more, but still want to come back because the learning is that good and productive. (p.43)

When in a safe space of coming to learn and unlearn, there must be a consideration and anticipation of the many ways that this might occur. What happens when one rejects one-dimensional terms and quick fixes for truly interrogating whiteness and racial domination? What potentialities might arise when taking a deep dive and committing to immersing oneself in concepts and ways of learning and being that require staying in the conversation? What might happen when unsettling and challenging complicity and its connection with upholding racist structures and systems that benefit those who identify and are racialised as white? How does critical reflexivity connect with educating for critical consciousness and learning critical theory? Finally, in what capacity does critical self-reflexivity allow for theoretical concepts to be humanised in ways that seek to challenge and interrogate how the hegemony of whiteness and racial domination are operationalised?

Conclusion

Critical self-reflexivity and educating for critical consciousness have the potential to activate radical thinking and liberation when it comes to teaching, learning, and unlearning. By understanding oneself as a racialised being through standpoint and positionality, possibilities arise that can challenge systems and individual behaviours that reinforce and/or uphold racial domination and white supremacy. However, there must be a move to sit with the discomfort that comes when working through processes that often leave one feeling less than positive about themselves.

To restate, white people do not always see the structures of power that they benefit from. Careful attention must be paid to the extent that whiteness intersects with other aspects of one's identity, and further shapes how one understands their roles within both education and society (White, 2012). Additionally, white people often desire to become 'good' and racially enlightened people, which without an awareness of what it means to centre whiteness, results in upholding and reinforcing racial domination and white supremacy. Going through this process is an epistemological exploration, or an exercise in reflexive mental gymnastics that aims to name and unsettle one's relationship to race and whiteness, both in broad and narrow senses. I hope that the remainder of this book provides an opportunity to experience the process of critical self-reflexivity and educating for critical consciousness, recognising the power and transformative potential that these two practices have when untangling whiteness and its relationship to education, resistance, and transformation.

Chapter 2

Critical Theory and Intersectionality

Introduction

Last year, in one of my 100-level sociology courses, a student raised their hand after I delivered a lecture on intersectionality and critical theory, and asked, "*Why does something need to be called critical theory for it to be taken seriously in the university? Why does this seem to be the only way that our experiences are validated?*" I'm so glad the student asked these questions, as they gave me an opportunity to explain the purpose of critical theory, and why it has the potential to be liberatory and transformative. As hooks (1994) argues,

> Theory is not inherently healing, liberatory, or revolutionary. It fulfils this function only when we ask that it do so and direct our theorising towards this end... [I] find writing and theoretical talk-to be most meaningful when it invites readers to engage in critical reflection and to engage in the practice of feminism... Personal testimony, personal experience, is such fertile ground for the production of liberatory feminist theory because it usually forms the base of our theory making (p.61/70).

For the remainder of the class, I talked about how experiences that are understood and explained as critical theory (or theoretical concepts) can provide a language and terminology that is communal and collective. It is deliberate and demands action and change. Through shared language, an experience becomes more than just a unique happening, or something that can be excused away as 'no big deal'. In this sense, critical theory can validate an experience, articulating it in a way that denotes an element of universality, albeit distinct as well. Significantly, critical theory is interconnected to one's standpoint and positionality, as it speaks to the often marginalised identity markers that have historically been and continue to be relegated to the sidelines Thus, critically theories that focus on race, feminist, queer, disability, (just to name a few) that centre these various identities, recognise the importance of coming to understand the world through diverse perspectives and experiences. Critical theories create a language that is emancipatory and grounded in activism and social change. This is the power and liberatory potential of critical theory.

The refusal and denial (both implicitly and explicitly) to see oppressive experiences as systematic and institutional is like stating 'racism is something that's happening over there, but definitely not here.' Within this perspective, one can become complicit in upholding various forms of marginalisation by questioning if something happened merely because it was not personally experienced. One can either hear and dismiss an experience as just an example of someone's individual lived reality, or they can work to make sense of it as their own experience *and* as part of the system that upholds and reproduces oppressive behaviour. Instead of considering such experiences as solely individualised, critical theory provides a framework in which to make sense of how they can be *both* individual *and* systemic. Thus, depending on lived experiences, standpoints and positionalities, everyone has different relationships with engaging, connecting, and making sense of critical theory. I seek to zoom out to zoom back in for a deeper analysis of society.

Critical theory, in the way I will be discussing throughout this chapter, builds on the practice of self-reflexivity, connecting it to action and transformation. I understand critical theory to be learnt proactively rather than something that should be memorised or mastered definitionally. Critical theory, through its connection to self-reflexivity, has the potential to aid in challenging various forms of oppression and marginalisation. It can also be used to enter a conversation that names something previously un-nameable. I've had students tell me that when they have the language and terminology to help explain concepts like race and whiteness, challenging discussions feel less contentious and daunting. Critical theory can be an entry point into a conversation, as it grounds difficult and heavy content with a term or phrase that helps explain and work to comprehend stories or experiences as systematic, rather than seeing them as just a one-off.

The purpose of this chapter is to bring together critical theories that help situate intersectionality as a *framework* and *lens.* As the previous chapter highlighted the importance of connecting standpoint, positionality, and various identities with the learnings of race and whiteness, I engage this chapter by focusing on the ways in which to unpack and deploy intersectionality as a theoretical framework and lens. Comprised of diverse critical theories, intersectionality speaks to the multiple ways to make sense of education and society; individually, structurally, and institutionally. The benefit and power of connecting with an intersectional framework and lens is that nothing can be taken for granted.

What does it mean to deploy something as a framework and lens? A framework zooms out and recognises that there are many ways to interpret or make sense of something. A framework is like a web, in that there is more than one explanation to unpack and analyse an event, setting, policy, practice, etc. Zooming back in, one can deploy a lens for a closer look. Think about putting glasses on. Due to their laser focus and intense prescription, glasses can serve as lenses that allow one to see something in depth, which prior to wearing the glasses, would have been visible, but now, is hyper-visible. Throughout this chapter, I demonstrate the importance of understanding that behaviours and ways of experiencing and interpreting the world are not happenstance nor are they accidental.

True to its namesake, intersectionality intertwines the various ways that one identifies, reinforcing how their interconnectivity directly relates to how one experiences and moves about the world. As such, I draw on a variety of scholars and critical theories within disciplines such as gender studies, queer theory, philosophy, disability studies, sociology, education, among others. Each theoretical interpretation is conceptualised as a web of interconnecting ideas, experiences, and knowledges that make up intersectionality and its relationship to education and society writ large.

Engaging with intersectionality as a framework and trying to make sense of it as a lens can feel abstract. Thus, I draw on three specific tenets that emerge out of the critical theories I deploy, as they have the potential to situate what intersectionality *is* and *how* it connects with making sense of something in a different way. Albeit from diverse disciplinary perspectives, the scholars and critical theories I draw from speak to intersectionality and its relationship to analysing education and society: *Questioning Hegemonic Forms of Oppressions, Disrupting the Education Canon, and Recognising Diverse Modes of Resistance.* First, I briefly define and discuss intersectionality as a term.

What is Intersectionality?

Crenshaw coined the metaphor in 1980's Manhattan. Whose roads are these? Who designed the grid, and then who built them? Whose land is the entire structure on? How does the grid itself marginalise people, transforming some people into so-called 'minorities' in the imperial gaze while supposedly being able to serve the interests of the 'majority'? For me these are the most productive questions that arise as we try to think about the relationship between intersectionality and marginality (Khatun, p.18, as cited in Silverstein, 2017).

In 1989, legal scholar Kimberlė Crenshaw, wrote a paper arguing that the outcome of three different legal cases[1] demonstrated the United States Court of Appeals Ninth Circuit's narrow definition of discrimination regarding a single issue analysis. Crenshaw articulated that the law seemed to forget that Black women are both Black and female, and thus subjected to discrimination on the basis of both race, gender, and often, a combination of the two. Crenshaw argued, "by treating black women as pure women or purely black, the courts, as they did in 1976, have repeatedly ignored specific challenges that face black women as a group"(Crenshaw as cited within Coaston, 2019. p.5). Crenshaw iterated that the courts failed, as they were only able to see that racism was what happened to Black people across genders, and that sexism was what happened to all women (regardless of race). Through such a narrow prism, there was no framework for Black women and Women of Colour to discuss and challenge multiple forms of discrimination. What emerged from this paper was the term *intersectionality*.

Although Crenshaw is known as the modern founder of intersectionality, Sojourner Truth, Black feminist, and activist, engaged in an intersectional framework almost two centuries before Crenshaw coined the term. Sojourner Truth, born Isabella Baumfree into slavery in 1787 in New York, was sold multiple times before marrying and becoming a mother. In 1827, Isabella refused to run away in secret, and instead, walked away by daylight after her master broke his promise to set her free. After she left, Isabella became a traveling Methodist preacher, changing her name to Sojourner Truth. Her activism led her to the 1851 Women's Rights Convention, where she delivered the ground-breaking speech '*Ain't I Woman*?' Throughout her speech, Truth refused to choose between abolition and feminism, proclaiming that "her blackness did not override her femaleness and advancing women's rights at the expense of the abolitionist movement wasn't an option."(Zamalin, 2019) At the heart of Truth's message was that the manner she engaged resistance was one that was truly intersectional.

---

[1] See DeGraffenreid v. General Motors, Moore v. Huges Helicopter, Inc. and Payne v. Travenol for further reading. https://openjurist.org/708/f2d/475/moore-v-hughes-helicopters-inc-a-division-of-summa-corporation

Over the last decade, intersectionality has become somewhat of a buzzword since the inauguration of Donald Trump in 2016. There was quite a lot of criticism about the planning and organising of the Women's March on Washington[2] once Trump was elected president of the United States. However, because of the term intersectionality, a deeper understanding of the tensions within the movement helped shift the conversation from thinking about feminism as a white, liberal, cisgender, heterosexual, able-bodied, middle/upper-class movement, to one that must be better understood as a framework to interrogate the historical and present 'norm' of what defines a feminist.

Definitionally, intersectionality focuses on social inequalities by highlighting power imbalances, as well as deep structural and systemic forms of discrimination. It is based on the premise that everyone simultaneously occupies multiple social positions, and that these positions do not cancel each other out, but instead, interact in complex ways that must be explored and understood (DiAngelo, 2012). Drawing from critical theories of race, whiteness, education, and feminism, (among others) intersectionality explores the interaction between different identity markers, such as race, gender, sexuality, etc., that underpin social, political, and economic formal rules and informal norms and cultures (Evans, 2016). Intersectionality moves away from seeing people as a homogenous, undifferentiated mass. Instead, it provides a framework for explaining how social divisions position people differently in the world (Collins and Bilge, 2016).

Intersectionality, as a framework, draws on a variety of critical theoretical interpretations that highlight intersecting oppressions, oppositional knowledges, and modes of disruption. Intersectional theory is necessarily equipped to be liberatory beyond the confines of the classroom community. Within the context of teaching and learning, intersectionality pushes back on the homogenising and hierarchical ways that students are taught to conceptualise epistemologies in the neoliberal university for the sake of valuing individual self-improvement,

---

[2] The Huffington Post sat down with two of the 2017 Women's March Organizers Linda Sarsour and Tamika Mallory. They discussed the notion that although conversations about intersectionality and the dangers of white feminism isn't new, the 2017 march brought such concerns back to the forefront. The event's initial organizers were criticized for naming the rally the Million Women's March, essentially taking the name of demonstrations that were organized by black activists in the mid-1990s. The organizers renamed the event and reached out to women of colour to help lead the event, but some women still remained sceptical (Gebreyes, R. *Huffington Post,* 1/27/17).

efficiency, job market viability and quantifiability (Davies & Bansel, 2007; Labaree, 1997). Critical theory as drawing from lived experience in this way, is socially, politically and materially useful for shaping transformative action, as well as for being able to recognise radical practises that are already happening (de Saxe & Trotter-Simons, 2021).

Most important, intersectionality offers a way to move beyond empathy (putting oneself in the others' shoes), which too often can result in being self-referential and centring whiteness, patriarchy, heteronormativity, etc. Rather, one may better understand an intersectional 'self' and an 'other' as interconnected, co-entangled and co-constructed which are ultimately bound by complex webs of oppression and liberation (Perry & Shotwell, 2009). An intersectional analysis provides a way to understand the relational sense of being intimately connected to one's social situatedness, affective understandings/knowledge (felt sense) and how this may aid in better understanding the personal, interpersonal, and structural-political levels and one's accountability within them. In other words, intersectionality has the potential to provide a way for one to make sense of where their individuality ends and their co-dependence with others begins.

Within such a nuanced and context-specific understanding, it shouldn't be a surprise to see the benefits of utilising an intersectional framework when aiming to challenge a single story of oppression and marginalisation within the context of education and society. To reiterate, critical theory provides a language in which to think about something in a different way. Because of this, the application and analysis of critical theory is more important than its definition, as intersectionality (comprised of diverse critical theories) is constantly under construction, malleable, and context-specific. In fact, intersectionality, as a framework and lens, require that close attention be paid to the historical, intellectual, and political contexts that shape what one thinks and does.

What follows is a discussion of three tenets that situate intersectionality within education: *Questioning Hegemonic Forms of Oppression, Disrupting the Educational Canon, and Recognising Diverse Modes of Resistance.* I engage each tenet as a specific way to consider and make sense of intersectionality as a framework. Each tenet may also be thought of as its own lens, focusing on something specific, that, at first glance, might not elicit the need for a deep analysis. However, when deploying a purposeful lens, the various dimensions of oppression and marginalisation surface. Significantly, although discussed independently, all three tenets interconnect with one another, recognising that they must be understood and attended to simultaneously. It is helpful to think about each tenets as a head of the hydra from Greek mythology. When attacking the hydra, if one head is cut off, another head (usually more) grows back in its place. Only when all the heads are slain at the same time, can the hydra be defeated (Theoi Project). Consider this story throughout the reading of this chapter. All the tenets (or heads) need to be understood and unpacked together through an intersectional framework, noting how they rely upon one another to expose, challenge, and interrupt all forms of marginalisation and oppression simultaneously.

Questioning Hegemonic Understandings of Oppression

The student reflections peppered throughout this chapter speak to the power of language and concepts, noting how they allow one to feel validated when sharing their experiences of oppression, whilst providing a platform in which to think about experiences that are different than one's own. The feeling of being part of a collective due to similar experiences does not imply that all forms of oppression are the same. The validation of knowing that others may have been subjected to oppressions like one's own is far from suggesting that generalisations should be made about experiencing any type of marginalisation. Every story is different, but each is part of a structure and system that upholds whiteness, racial domination, sexism, patriarchy, heteronormativity, ableism, etc. Thus, at its core, intersectionality avoids essentialist narratives about whom or what intersectionality is referring to. There is no universality in terms of how one experiences oppression and marginalisation.

Too often, speaking out and sharing stories of discrimination flatten differences by collapsing people who are marginalised into 'commonalities' of oppression among minoritised people and communities. The flattening of difference counsels out the practice of engaging standpoint and positionality, as it assumes that one's lived experience of being oppressed must be the same as others within their identity group. This couldn't be less true, as intersectionality speaks to various identities and diverse experiences, reinforcing that even those with a shared racial and/or feminist (among others) standpoint often have quite different positionalities.

Within this context, intersectionality as framework and lens leaves the conversation open to avoid narratives that generalise. Instead, intersectionality embraces and requires complexity, as its theoretical definition is constantly under construction, nuanced, and multi-dimensional. Speaking to this, Zakaria (2022) challenges the concept of binaries (something that is either/or) as well as one-dimensional identities. She argues for the importance of paying close attention to one's various identifications, noting how they intimately connect with experiencing diverse forms of marginalisation. In as much, intersectionality is undergirded with a philosophy and understanding that there is not just one way to define oppression. Only by learning, listening, and understanding the diversity of our lives and experiences, can there be a move away from seeing oppression as hegemonic, or as something that is universally experienced.

Intersectionality is also women-centred, collectivist and grounded in lived experiences (Moosa-Mitha, 2005). This approach to research privileges the specific and the contextual. In fact, to fully understand diverse modes of oppression, there must be a move away from validating positivist academic knowledges and 'T'ruths, and instead, base a critical feminist theory upon lived experiences and oppositional social movements. When conducting research, feminist theorists position the researcher and the participant in engaged and self-reflexive activities. Thus, rather than making universal claims, feminist researchers are working to make sense of their social realities through subjectivities that are based on narratives, performance, as well as other methodologies that incorporate individual, personal, and collective knowledges.

Revisiting the importance of racial and feminist standpoint, Collins (2000) argues that as a collective, Black women have been dehumanised and subjected to various forms of oppression: economic, political, and ideological. She notes, "while common experiences may predispose Black women to develop a distinctive group consciousness, they guarantee neither that such a consciousness will develop among all women nor that it will be articulated as such by the group" (p. 24). Further, as part of a true feminist struggle, hooks argues, "Black women recognise the special vantage point (our) marginality gives (us) and makes use of this perspective to criticise the dominant, racist, classist, sexist hegemony as well as to envision and create a counter-hegemony" (p. 43, 1986). hooks calls for the making of a liberatory feminist theory and praxis that undeniably depends on the unique and valuable experiences of Black women. hooks also emphasises the importance of paying attention to the various and diverse ways that women experience oppression. She not only resists a hegemonic interpretation of feminist thought by insisting that it is a theory in the making, but that we must also critique, question, and re-examine new possibilities.

In as much, the space of subjectivity, lived experiences, and critical race theory[3] also play a pivotal role in understanding the multidimensionality of an

---

[3] Critical race theory will be analysed in more depth in chapter 5.

intersectional framework. Critical race theory is underpinned by story-telling and counter-narratives that provide a powerful vehicle for speaking out and undermining racism. Critical race theory challenges the cultural scripts that state individualism, equal opportunity, and success are available for everyone. Within this perspective, Bhandar (2000) argues that feminist interventions in critical race theory have been crucial in shaping and developing a legal discourse that recognises the intersectionality of race, class, and gender (among others) formations.

Significantly, intersectionality and critical feminist theory provide an opportunity to better access the complexities of the world and of oneself. Collins and Bilge (2016) note that there are many ways that oppressions intersect and reinforce social divisions in each society at any given time. They both build on each other and are mutually inclusive. To reiterate, not only is it vital to consider multiple viewpoints and perspectives, but self-reflexivity, and the consideration of one's positionality and standpoint are further components of questioning multiple forms of oppression and their hegemonic interpretations. Understanding the interconnectivity of education and society requires a recognition of the entirety of oneself to challenge dominant ideologies of traditional educational practices, as well as tease apart universalised understandings of oppression and resistance. As hooks (1986) iterates, "women must learn to accept responsibility for fighting oppressions that may not directly affect (us) as individuals. When (we) show (our) concern for the collective, (we) strengthen (our) solidarity" (p. 137). To experience solidarity, there must be a community of interests, shared beliefs and goals around which to unite and build sisterhood. Within this perspective, I discuss *felt analysis*, a term deployed by critical Indigenous scholar Dian Million.

Million (2009) engages the term felt analysis to highlight Indigenous womens' personal experiences with colonisation and oppression through a racialised, gendered, and sexualised lens and perspective. Million describes felt analysis as a way for Indigenous women to participate in creating a new language and new narrative. She states:

> Felt analysis is a real multi-layered facet of histories and concerns by insisting on the inclusion of [our] lived experience, rich with emotional knowledge of what pain and grief and hope meant or mean now in [our] pasts and futures... the importance of felt experiences as community knowledges that interactively inform [our] positions as Native scholars (p.54).

Million argues that not only is felt experience often ignored, but its' very purpose is misconstrued and considered a subjective form of narrative, thus undermined and delegitimised "except in Western sciences own wet dream of detached corporeality"(Million, p.73). This act of telling disrupts the very nature of Native and Indigenous women not only in their own communities, but also in relation to the way history has always been told, articulated, and deemed as 'T'ruth.

Further, Million argues that Native women are challenged and denied a space as legitimate holders of objectivity. The very existence of these stories presents an alternative to what is considered truth. Million quotes Armstrong, who states "we must continue the telling of what really happened until everyone, including our own peoples, understands that this condition did not happen through choice (Armstrong as cited within Million, 2018, p.64). Through the concept felt analysis, Million argues that those who are subjugated throughout history must tell their stories in order to break through the silence that has systematically distorted the real truth, and to challenge what she recognises as a 'past that stays neatly segregated from the present'. However, Million discusses how speaking out puts Indigenous women in a precarious situation in their goal to change things by challenging the existence of silence that marks their pain and experiences. She iterates, "to tell called for a re-evaluation of reservation and reserve beliefs about what was appropriate to say about your own family, your community" (p.56). The very act of interrogating Native and Indigenous women's rights can and often does, result in the men within their communities allying with none other than the colonisers themselves. As Million speaks of her own struggles, she is clear that she doesn't speak for all women in Indigenous communities. However, she does note that felt analysis may provide a space to weave within and connect to others in their particular contexts and communities. Thus, by understanding the intricacies that reinforce flattening difference and hegemonic understandings of oppression, it is clear that the concept of felt analysis may be deployed as another lens through which to discuss, name, and challenge various forms of marginalisation.

Finally, I draw on Disability Critical Race Theory (DisCRit) as it further articulates the multiple and diverse ways that oppression is experienced. From an intersectional perspective, DisCrit sits within the discipline of disability studies and scholarship on ableism. Disability studies interrogates the all-encompassing systems of discrimination that exclude people who live with developmental, medical, neurological, physical, and psychological disabilities (Annanmma et al., 2018). Drawing on ableism scholarship within the context of intersectionality broadly, and challenging hegemonic forms of oppression specifically, ableism functions to interrogate individual, institutional, and cultural spaces that advantage people who are temporarily able-bodied and disadvantage people who are differently abled.

Expanding on critical race and feminist theories, DisCrit is an explicitly intersectional framework that explores the collusive nature of race and disability (Annanmma et al., p. 53). DisCrit challenges the complex ways that racism and ableism manifest, particularly within educational institutions that uphold hegemonic labelling and the stereotyping of students. Otherwise known as 'racialised ableism', DisCrit challenges the assumption that disability and race are mutually exclusive, and reinforces how intimately connected they are. DisCrit argues that Black, Indigenous, and People of Colour are too often imagined to be less intelligent, relegating students to the margins, and labelling them as having a deficit.

To counter such demeaning narratives, DisCrit centres the voices of the marginalised through counternarratives, *testimonios,* and other forms of research that challenge and undermine dangerous assumptions and stereotypes. In fact, DisCrit sees those who talk back as knowledge generators who can author their own stories and create solutions to the inequities they face. Building on educating for critical consciousness, DisCrit engages *intellectual activism,* which deliberately challenges systems of oppression and other ways that institutions normalise stereotypes and assumptions about Black, Indigenous, and People of Colour with a disability (in the broad and narrow sense of the term). Intellectual activism refuses deficit, damaging, and incapable labelling. It exposes hidden ideologies and curricula by highlighting the agency of students that are differently -abled. To restate, education and society are inextricably linked. The stereotypes and assumptions that uphold and perpetuate various oppressions are often learnt and reinforced within educational communities. Thus, there must be an interrogation of how one comes to understand knowledge and why there needs to be a reinterpretation of narratives that are one-side, whitewashed, as well as any type of learning that presents a skewed version of history and contemporary society.

Disrupting the Educational Canon

The 'educational canon,' is a term that denotes the 'seminal' texts and scholars that are deemed to be foundational as well as esteemed as the most important thinkers of their time (in discipline-specific contexts). These scholars and texts are often universally (or rather, hegemonically) understood as part of the canon, and rarely are there questions or challenges regarding what denotes someone or something as part of the 'canon.' Who decides the canonical thinkers, as well as which texts to read and privilege? Within the context of critical theory and intersectionality, these questions get to the purpose of the second tenet (and lens) *disrupting the educational canon.*

Throughout history, whiteness has established itself as the norm that represents an authoritative and hierarchical mode of thought (think hegemony and 'T'ruth). Content is often taught in binaries, silos, and through a one-sided account or perspective. Reason is taught as the opposite of ignorance, scientific knowledge as superior to Indigenous knowledge, and professional history is prioritised and is seen in opposition or juxtaposition to oral mythologies, just to name a few (Kinchole and Steinberg, 2008). In order to challenge dominant epistemologies of western knowledge production, I draw on decolonising methodologies, which seek to undermine and disrupt 'universal knowledges'. Decolonising methodologies focus on unique and diverse perspectives, beginning with the premise that histories need to be retold and rewritten in order to push back on sanitised accounts of the past (Tuhiwai Smith-1999). Within a whited -washed version of education, as well as how 'T'ruth and 'K'nowledge are defined, what becomes the 'true history' of the world's diverse peoples in general, as well as minoritised groups in western society, is told through and from a white historiographical lens.

The colonial power of whiteness is also connected to the educational canon and what is deemed 'official knowledge'. As Kinchole argues, "as with any racial category, whiteness is a social construction in that it can be invented, lived, analysed, modified, and discarded" (2008, p.167). The way that history is taught, whose perspectives are included, and whose voices are heard determines what and whom is considered as being 'in' or 'outside' the canon. Even the term 'outside the canon' represents that if something is inside (assumed official), then something must be outside (assumed alternative/in opposition).

Indigenous ways of knowing and being have the potential to contribute so much to the educational experiences of all students (Kinchole &b Steinberg, 2008). However, because of the status quo and dominant epistemologies of western knowledge production, such ways of thinking about education are deemed irrelevant within the university (Denzin and Lincoln, 2008). Challenging the hegemony of the academy (and education in general), Indigenous methodologies are grounded in active resistance, focusing on the unique and diverse experiences of marginalised individuals and communities, with the intention of undermining the manner that 'universal knowledges' are both conceptualised and understood (Mohanty, 2013). Grande (2009) speaks further to this through the term *Red Pedagogy*. Red Pedagogy is fundamentally rooted in Indigenous knowledge and praxis, promotes an education for decolonisation, and is grounded in hope, just to name a few. Grande speaks to the importance of asking critical questions and engaging in dangerous discourse in order to 'unthink' one's colonial roots whilst striving for and rethinking democracy.

Within an Aotearoa New Zealand and Māori context, Naomi Simmonds (2011) discusses decolonising politics and learning through a concept called mana wāhine (roughly understood as Māori feminism). Significantly, decolonisation is a critical strand to any mana wahine analysis. Simmonds discusses the problematic nature of attempting to directly translate 'mana' and 'wahine.' Instead, she notes that the spiritual realities of Māori women are inextricable from their physical realities; therefore, spirituality discourses remain vital to any articulations of mana wahine. Simmonds argues, "from this standpoint, decolonisation is not about fragmentation resulting from colonisation, but about unlearning, disengagement, and strengthening Māori at multiple levels" (p.17). She further understands mana wahine as art, as theory, as method, and as practice. Simmonds also recognises and provides for this in-betweenness and enables the exploration of diverse Māori realities from a position of power rather than having to talk or write back. Mana wahine defines projects as they are made up of a constellation of social, political, and cultural discourses that inform and are informed by Māori women's lived realities, as they are a necessary space where mātauranga wāhine (Māori women's knowledges) are centralised and validated. Awatare (1984) further argues that the role of the state in marginalising mana wahine knowledges cannot be stressed enough. As such, mana wahine provides another lens to engage with the on-going resistance movements that aim to decolonise the state, education, and dominant epistemologies (Penehira et al., 2014).

Another form of critiquing western forms of knowledge production within the academy is a practice called *multilogicality*. Per Kinchole & Steinberg (2008), multilogicality reinforces the need for students to encounter multiple perspectives when learning about historical and contemporary ideas. Teaching from a multilogical perspective provides a nuanced way to understand social analyses, political perspectives, and knowledge production. By incorporating multiple viewpoints and ways of being and seeing the world, multilogical educators begin to look at teaching from the perspectives of individuals from different races, classes, genders, abilities, and sexual orientations (among others) and are dedicated to searching for new perspectives.

Challenging a one- sided and dominant account of history has always been part of bringing subjugated knowledges from the margins to the centre. Ida B. Wells (1862-1931), activist and seminal African American sociologist, spent her life challenging, reframing, and retelling what was disseminated as 'T'ruth. Wells flipped the script on the narrative of history just after the 14th amendment (providing all citizens equal protection under the law) was passed in 1868. Speaking as a Black woman facing double discrimination, Wells told the true account of the violence, persecution, and the ways that Black men were framed as inherently evil and to be feared (Zamalin, 2019). Her activism and challenging the way history is told still resonates today and speaks to current resistance movements that interrogate anti-Black racism and white supremacy in the United States and around the world. In fact, the Black Lives Matter statement at Western Washington University states:

> The long history of the Black Radical Tradition compels us to question state narratives and to use the tools we have to speak truth to power. Ida B. Wells' work demands that we interrogate the 'excuses' that are given to erase extrajudicial executions and that we name the falsehoods. Wells shows us that we must listen to the communities that are affected and we must act. State violence against the black community is part of a centuries long practice that must end (Western Washington University website, 2023).

Through this reframing, interrogating, and relearning of what counts as 'T'ruth and 'K'nowledge, education can be unsettled and challenged. Through an intersectional framework that focuses specifically on disrupting the educational canon, a one-sided account of history and western knowledge production are exposed by challenging power, hierarchy, and status. Situating this tenet inside educational institutions is just one of the many ways that intersectionality engages with various modes of resistance. What follows is a multi-dimensional discussion of conceptualising and actualising resistance. When looking at intersectionality as a framework, there must be a variety of ideas and means by which to challenge, undermine, and resist.

Recognising Diverse Modes of Resistance

There are infinite ways to talk about and engage resistance and action. Resistance can be confrontational. It can be uncomfortable. Resistance can be many things, but one characteristic that is universal is that resistance is deliberate and intentional. Intersectionality as a framework underscores the importance of conceptualising resistance as direct, multi-faceted, and nuanced. Thus, when complicating and considering the many ways that resistance is situated within an intersectional framework, it is helpful to engage the following two guiding questions: *1) What kind of society do we want? and 2) Can we imagine a society that brings us closer to an unequivocally better world?* (Suissa, 2010). What might a reconceptualisation of education and society look like through an intersectional lens, and how might one better understand the diverse and various ways to resist? Through a discussion and lens of *recognising diverse modes of resistance,* I draw on a few critical scholars, namely within critical feminist theory, to unpack and conceptualise the diversity of resisting and disrupting.

At its core, critical feminist theory is constantly interrogating and unsettling an entire interconnected system, ultimately aiming towards liberation, emancipation, and empowerment. Critical feminist theory embodies critical and difference-centred perspectives and continues to evolve as a framework that responds to injustices and marginalisations. Cannella and Manuelito (2008) understand feminist research, conceptualisations and practices as wide ranging, complex, and constituting the diversity of human beings. They consider the role of feminism as a way to understand the term 'social justice' from a variety of standpoints, aiming towards creating transformative solidarities that offer possibilities for collective work across diversity. Although critical feminist theory is malleable and multi-dimensional, there are a few 'pivot points' that ground one's thinking about how it may be deployed as a framework or mode of resistance. Dadds (2011) considers the following pivot points for transformative action: reflexive historicity, lived experience and hidden structures, dialogic engagement with the margins, and embodiment and interdependence. These pivot points serve as key feminist contributions to critical social theory and resistance, as they pay close attention to interrogating society with a critical social feminist eye.

Feminist and queer scholar Audre Lorde (1984) approaches resistance by welcoming difference, rather than 'merely tolerating' people who are different. As resistance and activism have the potential to be communal and collective, difference (or those who are different than oneself) should be embraced because it is that which provides a fund of necessary polarities between which our creativity can spark like a dialectic. In fact, as Khatun argues, "rather than buying this story that theorises humans as deviations from a white, male, propertied, heterosexual, Protestant-but secular individual, [I] want to look at how the colonial production of these categories continues to see the very terms in which [we] talk about difference" (2017, p.16). In other words, activism and resistance should be conceptualised in a more nuanced and multi-faceted way, pushing back on assigned categories, as well as assumptions and stereotypes that work to separate and divide. Everyone is unique and is socially located within a system of power imbalances and categories that aim to keep one in their 'assigned' place and status within the hegemonic hierarchy of society. There must be a desire to reimagine communities as places that engage and understand the multidimensionality of resistance.

Drawing on and from the Combahee Rive Collective's *A Black Feminist Statement* (1978), I underscore the importance of resistance as it relates to the community and the collective. This particular work offers a powerful epistemological critique that discusses four major topics that address the following issues as they relate to intersectionality and resistance: 1) The genesis of contemporary Black feminism; 2) what (we) believe, i.e.., the specific province of our politics; 3) the problems in organising Black feminists, including a brief herstory of our collective; and 4) Black feminist issues and practice (Combahee River Collective, p.3). These specific ideas and concerns arouse out of the disillusionment and lack of resonance felt by many Black feminists during some of the liberation movements of the 1960s and 1970s. The Combahee River Collective needed more than the isolated modes of oppositional resistance practised politically at the time, ie, civil rights, black nationalism, the Black Panthers. The belief of the Combahee Rive Collective is that "the most profound and potentially the most radical politics come directly out of [our] own identity, as opposed to working to end someone else's oppression" (Combahee River Collective, p.5).

Considering the many ways that resistance can be conceptualised, both epistemologically and practically, I find it useful to draw on Sandoval (2000), who calls for a *differential consciousness*, or an alternative way in which to reassess current understandings of resistance and transformation. Sandoval recognises the various ways that race, gender, sexuality, and class intersect, arguing that for true oppositional resistance and action to materialise, they need to be engaged with simultaneously. Think back to the heads of the hydra; they must all be slain concurrently so that the monster can be defeated. Similarly, an intersectional framework of resistance requires that close attention is paid to all facets of oppression, aiming towards interrogating, challenging, and working to dismantle all of them at once.

As solidarity and self-reflexivity are intimately connected to intersectionality and its relationship to resistance, it is appropriate to consider the practice of *relationality.* As defined by Collins and Bilge (2017), relationality is a commitment to the development of coalitions or relations across social divisions. They state, "relational thinking rejects either/or and binary thinking, for example, opposing theory to practice, scholarship to activism, or black to white" (p. 27). One cannot effectively move forward with resistance and disruption without attention and understanding of critical theory, as well as noting how one is connected to these theories, and that they are an extension of practice (and vice versa). The way I deploy and engage critical theories is from the premise they do not exist solely for analysing the experience of others, but they coexist within and through everyone (Saavedra and Pérez, 2012). These purposes are intimately connected to the various ways in which one can aim to resist and transform.

To underscore the importance of conceptualising resistance as multi-layered and multi-faceted, I look to José Muñoz (2009) scholar of queer theory. Muñoz interrogates heteronormativity by reframing and challenging dominant epistemologies within feminist thought. He reconsiders and unsettles hegemonic interpretations of concepts, methods, and theories within feminism that exclude queer and non-heteronormative perspectives. Muñoz deploys a methodology of hope, which he describes as "a backwards glance that enacts a future vision" (p.4). He sees a methodology of hope as an alternative way to reconceptualise queerness as more than simply a being or a state, but instead, as a matter of thinking about that thing (queerness) that allows one to feel this world is not enough, and that something is missing. Muñoz traverses throughout thought, time, and space, and deliberately moves away from the here and now. He calls for a utopia, or a conceptual reinterpretation of life as the 'not-yet conscious,' as well as a different way to consider queerness. Muñoz's queer futurity reimagines an awareness of the past to critique the present. In doing so, Muñoz argues that much of queer critique is antirational and antiutopian, thus there must be a push to think beyond the moment and be available to the not-yet-here. Per Muñoz, prescribed time and space must be turned upside down so that there can be a reimagination of a different and better future.

Drawing on another mode of resistance, I look to, Gloria Anzaldúa (1987 & 1997) scholar of feminism, race, and queer studies. Anzaldúa also situates her work through place and belonging, and intersecting identities. Termed *borderlands feminism,* she articulates her sense of self as if she is caught between two cultures whilst simultaneously feeling like an imposter in both. Anzaldúa compares her experience to that of two worlds merging to form a third country, a border culture. She describes her experience as a cultural collision. Anzaldúa states:

Being lesbian and raised Catholic, indoctrinated as straight, I made the choice to be queer. It's an interesting path, one that continually slips in and out of the white, the Catholic, the Mexican, the indigenous, the instincts. It is path of knowledge-one of knowing (and of learning) the history of oppression of our raza. It is a way of balancing, of mitigating duality (p. 19).

By engaging Anzaldúa and her framing of borderlands feminism, I reinforce the importance of identities and how they are situated with the political, historical, and social, noting their interconnectivity to power, domination, and the upholding of social inequities.

Relatedly, underpinning diverse modes of resistance is a focus on interrupting and challenging whiteness. Ahmed (2017) unsettles both whiteness and patriarchy through her policy of citational practices. Ahmed does not draw on and/or cite scholarship from 'white men' throughout her feminist and critical race analyses. To clarify, Ahmed does, in fact, cite multiple white male scholars, but she makes a point to note that she refers to a 'white man' as an institution, not an individual (although both are often true). In other words, the white men Ahmed engages and cites throughout her work interrogate and interrupt patriarchy, racism, queerness, and white supremacy, among other forms of marginalisation. Similarly, Zakaria (2022) critiques white feminists who refuse to consider the ways that whiteness and racial privilege play in universalising feminism. Zakaria (2022) states,

You do not have to be white to be a white feminist. It is also perfectly possible to be white and feminist and not be a white feminist. The term describes a set of assumptions and behaviours which have been baked into mainstream Western feminism, rather than describing the racial identity of its subjects (p,xi).

Awatere (1984) also undermines and disrupts white-centric feminism. She argues that for white women, their first loyalty is to white culture and a white way of being. Awatere states, "the oppressor avoids confronting the role they play in oppressing others" (p.42). Loyalty is seen as a rejection of the sovereignty of Māori and in their acceptance of the imposition of British culture on Māori. Awatere argues that justice for Māori women does not exist without Māori sovereignty. She further reinforces the interconnecting facets of understanding feminist issues: Māori language, land rights, the hatred of Māori by Pākehā. All these forms of resistance intersect with feminism from a Māori perspective.

Of importance, resistance is individual, communal, context and location specific. It is personal and political. Resistance includes learning critical theory, marching in the streets, talking back through personal testimonies, informally and formally challenging others in writing and activist work (among many others). There is no one way to engage in resistance and disruption. This versatility is that manner that Johanna Hedvah (2020) embodies resistance. Hedvah, author of *Sick Woman Theory*, reframes understanding of chronic illness and wellness. They discuss the problematic nature of equating political protest with visibility, noting that for people with chronic illness, protest looks and is experienced differently, often behind the scenes and out of the public. Hedvah further redefines the concept of existence in a body as something that is primarily and always vulnerable. Reinforcing gender as a social construct, Hedva uses the term 'woman' to represent the institution of a 'woman.' Just as Ahmed characterises white men both individually and institutionally, Hedva's attention to the term woman follows suit. 'Woman' represents the un-cared for, the secondary, the oppressed, the non- the un- the less than. In other words, anyone who is oppressed and marginalised by whiteness, patriarchy, sexism, transphobia, ableness, wellness, etc. is conceptualised as a sick woman. Given the way that activism and resistance work can often be performative, policed, and critiqued, I include Hedvah's discussion of sick woman theory, as it is provocative, necessary, and timely in our current moment.

The purpose of *recognising diverse modes of resistance* as a lens within intersectionality is to highlight the importance of engaging with and drawing from feminist, queer, and critical race scholars that centre voices and perspectives traditionally undermined and relegated to the margins. When considering diverse modes of resistance, I deploy ideas and theories that seek to expose and interrupt multiple forms of oppression and marginalisation. What all the scholars I include throughout this chapter (among others not discussed here) demonstrate is that all spaces are political, radical theory and insurgent knowledge can be reframed, and that there is a 'feminist killjoy' (Ahmed, 2017) that resides within each and everyone.

Conclusion

And every now and then, the possibilities explode. In these moments of rupture, people find themselves members of a 'we' that did not until then exist, at least not as an entity with agency and identity and potency; new possibilities suddenly emerge, or that old dream of a just society re-emerges and---at least for little while-- shines (Solnit, p. xxv, 2016).

As Collins (2000) discusses, the notion of intersecting oppressions considers the macro and micro level ways that experiences of marginalisation uphold systems and structures that reinforce inequality. Thus, the theoretical is intimately connected to the individual and the collective, which also intersects with action, transformation, and resistance. However, there must be an active and acute awareness to not collapse social categories and oppressions. Instead, the nuances of intersectionality aim to capture the diversity (in many senses of the term) of identities and their relationship to power and oppression; both institutionally and individually. Intersectionality understands and analyses each inequality separately as well as simultaneously.

To reiterate, education and society are intimately linked. Both incorporate and embody many ideas, theories, and knowledges from interdisciplinary and diverse communities. Thus, when learning about intersectionality as a framework and lens, I seek to make sense of its relationship to transforming education and society. Intersectionality engages diverse perspectives and experiences of oppression, analyses the sociocultural and socio-political conditions that play out within education and society, as well as draws on a variety of ways to resist. Each tenet discussed throughout this chapter recognises the potentialities of intersectionality and its relationship to actualising liberatory education and beyond. However, per the ethos of intersectionality, there must be a commitment to challenging both the overt and institutionalised forms of whiteness, racism, sexism, ableism, heteronormativity (among others) that are so fundamentally present within education and society.

Intersectionality and its incorporation and inclusion of critical theory share three similarities: they draw from the broader philosophical traditions of participatory democracy, work primarily in schooling and formal educational institutions as one location for their praxis; and aim towards navigating differences as an important part of developing a critical consciousness (Collins and Bilge, 2016). Unquestionably, conceptualising the many facets of intersectionality discussed thus far demonstrates the steep hill that lies ahead. Challenging the notions of oppression, individualism, and self-meritocracy requires a significant reframing and shift in understanding the very essence of education and society. This is where I move from engaging intersectionality and critical theory as frameworks and lenses, to discussing how they might be used as tools for action and resistance. The next three chapters speak specifically to interrupting the 'white university,' describing how to deploy and activate tools of resistance which have the potential to untangle, expose, and work towards education and transformation.

PART 2

A Three-Pronged Approach for Disruption

Throughout chapters one and two, I reinforced the importance of situating racial standpoint, positionality, and their various relationships to the content of this book. I also unpacked the many ways that one may come to understand intersectionality and critical theory as a framework and lens. As discussed, theory isn't inherently healing in and of itself, but it has the potential to be so when deployed in ways that humanise and centre experiences that are often relegated to the margins. However, even this statement can feel abstract without knowing where and how to direct such theorising, in addition to how it can connect to action and liberation.

When I first started teaching at the university, students would often share that they felt stuck in their thinking and writing about the critical theory we engaged. They expressed a sense of being overwhelmed by the magnitude of some of the theories and concepts and their relationships with and to them. Students still express similar sentiments, and articulate that they know what they want to write about, but are unsure of how to frame their ideas in ways that meaningfully interconnect the theory and concepts as central to their main argument and analysis. Students also discuss their struggle to connect theory and action, as well as how this interconnectivity can lead to resistance (i.e., praxis). In other words, students want to bring theory into their writing, but are unsure how to do so. Thus, what emerged over the years is a process I call a 'three-pronged approach'. A three-pronged approach considers the following questions: 1) What is the 'problem', 2) What is upholding the 'problem', and 3) How might one respond to, work to transform, and/or attempt to challenge the 'problem'? These three questions situate and activate theory in ways that have the potential to interrupt and transform. In essence, the three-pronged approach assists in zooming out to understand the macro (the bigger picture) to zoom back in and engage the micro (something specific within the big picture). The first question gets to the issue at hand, the second deploys some theoretical concepts and ideas that speak to *why* the problem exists, is upheld, and persists, and the third question provides an opportunity to consider resistance, disruption, and even transformation as it relates to undermining the problem.

Throughout the next three chapters I engage some ideas and concepts within this three-pronged approach. Specifically, I unsettle the 'white university' philosophically and theoretically (the problem), how the 'white university' persists and is reproduced through diversity and colour-blindness (what upholds the problem), and finally, how critical race theory and *testimonio* have the potential to resist and disrupt (challenging and transforming the problem). I find that drawing on this three-pronged approach helps to humanise and focus specifically on one element of a larger picture, thus providing an opportunity to unpack it in its entirety, ultimately working to undermine it. Throughout this process, interrogating and challenging whiteness and racial domination within the university becomes something more concrete and focused, with the goal of working towards deliberate transformation and resistance.

Chapter 3

What is the 'White University'? (Three-pronged approach question 1: What is the problem?)

Introduction

Education and society are inextricably linked, and are underpinned by privileging whiteness and upholding racial domination. What happens in the classroom (beginning from early childhood all the way through university) is just a microcosm of how society functions as it perpetuates systems of stark inequality and oppression. Behaviour in the community is learnt and reproduced in the classroom and vice versa. In fact, the first time young people can 'respond' to stereotypes and 'engage' in how identities are socially constructed is at school: the playground, learning spaces that may be grouped by ability, philosophies of school and learning, funding allocation, curriculum, etc. These ideas spill over into society and are reinforced through systems of racial domination and ideologies of whiteness.[1] Seminal and prolific philosopher of race and whiteness Charles Mills argues that within these systems (such as education and society), there are rules, as well as pre-set expectations of social interactions and behaviours that are interconnected as a matrix and/or web. The only way to dismantle the omnipresent nature of whiteness and racial domination within and beyond education, is to recognise that both exist as a complex web that is comprised of philosophies, policies, and rules that are socially agreed and acted upon.

When I begin a lecture speaking about the 'white university,' I explain to students that I don't mean this in the literal sense, (although most students I teach identify and are socialised as white) but rather in a philosophical,

---

[1] I follow Burke's (2017) definition of ideology as being always grounded in material realities, embedded in institutions and concrete social practices that give them meaning and produce real social outcomes... ideologies are racist to the degree that they maintain a racialised social system.

institutional, and structural sense. I find that by interconnecting the following three theoretical concepts *Racial Contract, Historical Privilege, and Education Debt*, students can situate and make sense of the 'white university' philosophically, so as to untangle how it manifests in reality: i.e., the problem. This is a difficult exercise, as whiteness (as well as racial domination) are so deeply embedded in these theories and philosophies that they are often hard to see and name directly. Anticipating this challenge, I ask students to think about how they understand and personally connect with some of the ideas after the lecture. I give them ten minutes or so to journal where they are in terms of making sense of the 'white university,' as well as how the concepts resonate within their own lives. Pedagogically, I appreciate these reflections as they prepare me for what I might need to explain in greater detail in the following lecture. More importantly, though, the student reflections give me an opportunity to better understand how they personally connect with their initial learnings about the 'white university'. Below I share a student's reflection (paraphrased and anonymised) after the lecture on the Racial Contract, Education Debt and Historical Privilege.

> I often think about what prompts people to ask me if I am from a 'fancy suburb.' I think they do this because being Māori, the assumption is that there is no way I can actually be from that suburb. They seem surprised when I say yes, as if they didn't even realise that what they were asking was so that they could racially categorise me. After the lecture on the Racial Contract, Education Debt and Historical Privilege, I had a realisation that they do this because they believe that we only belong in certain spaces, and are only to be certain people, and they are allowed to belong **everywhere** and be **whomever** they want, because that's how society constructs it to be. Another thing I thought about was how Pākehā respond when we don't fulfil their ideas of who they think we are, or that we don't belong in the spaces that are mapped out for us. We are often singled out as an exception to the rule rather than an opportunity for them to reassess the preconceived ideas of who we are. We become not like your 'usual' Māori.

Setting the Stage

The purpose of this chapter is to zoom out so that I can conceptualise and theorise the 'white university,' discussing how it is a 'problem.' Coming from the premise that whiteness is so institutionalised within the structures of the university, it is often taken for granted and understood as an individual problem rather than something that is systemic and structural. Pushing back on this one-dimensional and under-developed interpretation, I ask and unpack the following questions: *What is the white university theoretically? What does it look like philosophically and institutionally?* Throughout this chapter, I discuss how the white university is not accidental nor is it new. I situate these questions by analysing three different yet interconnected ideas, the Racial Contract, Historical Privilege, and the Education Debt. All three concepts uphold and maintain racial domination and the problematic nature of the white university.

This chapter challenges and complicates the many ways that whiteness manifests within university education. I draw on Mills' (1997, 2015) Racial Contract, Borrel et al. (2018) Historical Privilege, and Ladson-Billings's (2006) Education Debt, as all three speak to how power and privilege intersect, ultimately upholding ideologies and philosophies of whiteness within the university. As the three frameworks cross boundaries and work to uphold white supremacy around the world, I specifically draw on examples from Aotearoa, New Zealand and the United States to reinforce the importance of situating the sociocultural, political, and historical elements of whiteness, particularly within an educational context. Although I describe these conceptual frameworks independently, their mutual inclusivity is paramount to the sustainability of the white university. It is through a misinterpretation of the world that the Racial Contract, and by extension, Historical Privilege, and the Education Debt, are upheld and maintained. The metaphorical contract underpins each privilege and debt, as without institutionalised and structural whiteness, they would cease to exist.

Breaking through the Walls of Whiteness

Many white students enter university having minimal exposure beyond white neighbourhoods and experiences. This is likely due to increased and sustained segregation within many neighbourhoods throughout the United States but could also extend to neighbourhoods and institutions around the world. As a result, many students have little experience in classrooms that are racially, ethnically, and economically diverse, likely limiting their ability to perceive racial bias and negative stereotypes directed towards Black, Indigenous, and Students of Colour. These predispositions contribute to the prevalence and demonstration of racial apathy, as well as an avoidance in talking about race and whiteness in traditionally white spaces (Jakumar and Adamian, 2017). As Applebaum (2012) argues, "since contemporary forms of systemic racism are insidiously covert, conceptions of responsibility that cannot capture the subtle ways individuals are related to the perpetuation of such systems may themselves be implicated in preserving an unjust status quo" (p.618). Thus, to truly engage with resistance and substantive change, there must be a comprehensive understanding of the explicit and implicit ways that unexamined whiteness reinforces the inherent oppression found within our educational institutions and communities.

To make sense of this argument, I draw on Brunsma, Brown & Placier (2012) and their metaphor of the 'walls of whiteness:'

> Our white students believe the system *is* already just and do not actually *see a system* at all; they see a set of ideas that have been in place throughout the history of this nation and a set of relationless individuals who act out these historical ideas from their self-interest... part of this stems from their understanding of rights as political and civil and *not* social, cultural and economic, and the ideology of individualism (p.731).

The walls of whiteness symbolise a form of protection and comfort, which results in students closing themselves off from deliberately challenging whiteness within university classroom communities. Through my own experience teaching, learning, and researching within higher education, both in the United States and Aotearoa, New Zealand, I notice that deliberately interrogating racism and white supremacy is not something that is commonplace. Even for students who study within the social sciences and humanities, whiteness, and white supremacy are often danced around, glossed over, or ignored altogether. Although argued over twenty years ago by McIntyre (2002), the following statement still resonates; "Students are accustomed to a culture of niceness that often suffocates critique in many classrooms and institutions of higher learning…it is a significant barrier to developing a discourse that critically explores the various dimensions of whiteness" (p.44). If these topics are engaged with, they are done so in a cursory manner that often reinforces a binary and one-dimensional interpretation of how whiteness is upheld and reproduced.

Anecdotally, courses that discuss race and whiteness tend to do so with such content at the periphery as opposed to the 'critical' centre. By 'critical', I refer to whiteness being centred in a way that directly critiques and challenges it. In contrast, in education spaces that uncritically centre whiteness, students may learn about white privilege, which too often focuses on Peggy McIntosh (1990) and the 'knapsack,' thus understanding whiteness as experiencing individual privileges. Additionally, white students tend to reproduce whiteness as they discuss it. For example, although they may learn and discuss whiteness, seeking to understand it is as connected to maintaining systems of power and privilege, students often recentre it by doubling down on expressions and feelings of guilt and shame. This results in subversively and even insidiously recentring the very topic they were working to challenge and interrogate.

Within this surfaced and sometimes misguided context, students are not asked to actively consider their own culpability (both intentionally or unintentionally) in maintaining and upholding whiteness and racial domination. Students may solely focus their 'learning' on race and racism, leaving out how whiteness as an ideology is crucial to both maintaining and reproducing systems and institutions of whiteness. Through this glossing over the insidious ways that white supremacy works and is upheld, racial awareness *accommodates* rather than challenges structures of power that have the potential to alter the larger system of racism and racial ideology (Burke, 2017). As a result, the many ways that whiteness is maintained and reinforced become a disconnected concept as opposed to something that students may seek to understand as being both subversive and covert. Jayakumar and Adamian (2017) articulate this point well:

By absolving whites as beneficiaries of racism, colorblind frames notably shield whites from acknowledging institutional racism and white privilege. In adhering to the false notion that we live in a colorblind[2] society, whites are protected from feeling discomfort, shame, or personal responsibility for the realities of racism (p.915).

In other words, white people become indifferent to both the structural and everyday acts of whiteness. As Kelley and Yancy (2022) note, the spectacle of racism teaches white people the consequences of being Black or Brown but does not teach white people how this subverts the power of whiteness when it is not interrogated. Thus, the everyday expressions of institutional power are through racial education and racialisation of what it means to *not be white*. So little attention is paid to directly and deliberately interrogating whiteness and racial domination that many students can spend their entire tenure at university sidestepping such content altogether. As a result, too many students leave the university unprepared to challenge the many facets of white supremacy both within education and society. With this in mind, what follows is a discussion of Mills' Racial Contract, as it provides a framework to untangle

---

[2] Colour-blindness will be unpacked and analysed in chapter four.

the invisibility and normalising structures that make whiteness omnipresent within and beyond education.

The Racial Contract

The Racial Contract is an internalised tendency to produce a defined and agreed-upon pattern of behaviours and practices. White people have created a world that they, in general, will not understand (Kelley and Yancy, 2022). It is a creation that seeks to maintain a society steeped in white hegemony. In as much, the Racial Contract provides a specific framework to think about racial domination within the white university, as universities inherently make-up and reproduce whiteness. I begin with a description of Mills' Racial Contract (1997) via Leonardo (2015), whereby Leonardo critiques and challenges the maintenance of an inequitable, oppressive, and racist education system. Leonardo argues that the Racial Contract manifests within the broad field of education and society, reinforcing such notions as whiteness as an ideology, white supremacy, and hegemony.

Through the Racial Contract, (and within its subcontracts: *spatial, epistemological, and whiteness as bully*), the world and social order reinforce that it was/is written by and for whites, and that it functions to maintain their rights and standing of whiteness. There is a global reach of whiteness that is seen both within education and society. Mills (2015) emphasises the following point:

> While the 'Contract' is clearly false as a literal account, it can be regarded as a powerful and evocative figure for expressing two basic truths, one descriptive and one normative: that society is a human construct (not an organic growth, or a supernatural creation) and that human beings have an equality in the pre-social state of nature that should be preserved in the socio-political institutions they create once they leave it (p. 545).

What follows is a discussion of the spatial subcontract, epistemological subcontract, and whiteness as a bully. All three ideas rely upon one another to uphold a framework of whiteness and racial domination.

Spatial Subcontract

The spatial subcontract, which I conceptualise as a tentacle within the Racial Contract, pays close attention to the ways that space is upheld and reinforced through a white lens, habitus, and perspective. Language and its meanings become coded, reproducing one-dimensional understandings and privileging whiteness as the norm. Words such as 'safe neighbourhoods,' 'ghetto,' 'urban,' 'high performing,' 'at-risk,' all come with racialised and classed assumptions. It is not accidental that such words come with agreed-upon meanings that rely on stereotypes for 'universal' and hegemonic interpretations. These terms (just to name a few) are racially coded for black, brown, and white, the latter being the frame by which others should be measured against. Circling back to the student response above, they described the connection between the spatial subcontract and the questioning of the suburb they came from. The socially constructed assumption for who belongs and doesn't belong in certain neighbourhoods (and, by extension, schools) is on full display here. The 'fancy' neighbourhood (per the student's reflection) has been coded as white, thus their presence appeared 'unusual' or 'out of place.'

Within the spatial subcontract, the assumption about the world is that whiteness is the norm and that the right to be blind and complicit within a system of whiteness is embedded within the Contract. This subcontract also privileges hegemonic understandings of knowledge production, what is considered 'official knowledge,' or understood and disseminated as 'T'ruth (Apple, 2008). This is the perspective that is fed within an ideological framework of whiteness and power. Black, Indigenous and People of Colour are considered within a perspective of sub-personhood (they are treated as tabula-rasa; banking education; Freire 1974) to be filled with and consumed by white intentions. This manner of teaching and learning reinforces the assumption that measuring education and success through a white lens is the *only* lens as it is framed as incontestable. Within the context of academia in Aotearoa, New Zealand, Kidman (2019) argues, "Indigenous and minoritised Black faculty are frequently perceived as less able, less rational, less knowledgeable, and less 'civilised than white academics, providing them with a tacit basis for marginalising them" (p.4). Even if not explicitly stated, through the spatial contract, there is a hegemonic and agreed-upon stereotype for who is and can be an academic. Within this framing, the belief is that white academics are more credible and have a higher status than BIPOC academics.

Also embedded within the spatial subcontract is Ahmed's (2007) notion of whiteness taking up space. Ahmed's framing reinforces how the world of whiteness is implicit as a default or represents a normalised version of living comfortably in society. Yancy (2018) speaks to this through his letter *"Dear White America."* Throughout, Yancy asks his white readers to accept the racism within themselves. Specifically, he states, "What I'm asking is that you first accept the racism within yourself, accept all of the truth about what it means for you to be white in a society that was created for you...you have already signed the contract, so to speak, that guarantees you a certain form of social safety" (p.23). Who 'belongs' and who is perceived as not belonging denotes the inherent whiteness of a space. Again, the above student's response reinforces an agreed-upon understanding that white people feel comfortable and belong everywhere, whereas Black, Indigenous, and People of Colour are 'assigned' certain and specific spaces. When outside of these spaces, they are considered 'out of place,' reinforcing which spaces are for them and which spaces are not.

The spatial subcontract also understands colonisation as a 'natural process,' as it is assumed that a geographic location is not liveable until the initial inhabitants are pushed aside, eradicated, or assimilated. Society becomes 'established' once the colonisation process begins and continues. Countries such as New Zealand and New Caledonia (just to name two) were, and continue to be, colonised and must reckon with the consequences of existing (and resisting) as a settler colonial country. Kidman et al. (2018) add that the establishment of settler-colonial societies in far-off lands was justified by settler denial that any systems of governance would exist prior to colonisation. Within this context, the power of language is paramount to the sustainability of the spatial subcontract. Awatare (1984) argues,

> The political and economic power of the settlers was used to spread their own culture and values at the expense of Māori culture and values; the settlers' belief in their own cultural superiority prevented them from allowing Māori culture to exist side by side, preventing them from even learning our own language or wanting to forge a new national identity which included the Māori (p.13).

In Aotearoa, New Zealand, when the term monocultural (as opposed to bicultural) is deployed as a way to describe the country, the implication is that white New Zealanders have developed a culture that is particularly New Zealand in nature, reinforcing the assumption that the 'white culture' of Aotearoa is the norm and Māori culture, language, etc., is the 'other.'

Educationally, the spatial element of the subcontract is preserved through a neoliberal sorting machine, advocating streaming, test scores, and other standardised means to measure 'achievement,'[3] 'success,' and 'k'noweldge.

---

[3] Historically and presently, tracking, test scores, and measuring academic "achievement" often reinforces the deeply interconnected nature between classism, sexism, racism and ableism.

Criteria regarding majors chosen, content taught, as well as the status of disciplines, are often seen and ranked through an ideological framework of whiteness. They are particularly created to maintain and sustain whiteness and its many manifestations that normalise it as superior. Those who adhere to this neoliberal and ideological thinking circumvent any attention that would call out inequality (class, gender, racial, otherwise), working to quickly neutralise it or consider it passé (Darder, as cited within de Saxe, 2016). This dismissiveness reinforces a practice of 'othering,' whilst creating a climate of institutionalising inferiority, suggesting that those who do not subscribe to such standards internalise a sense that they are less than or are not achieving to a standard that is taken as a given for proficiency and achievement. Significantly, internalising and believing one's inferior status is also part of the spatial subcontract. As Mills argues, the contract is written and rewritten to uphold whiteness. Domination, acquiescence, and the maintenance of whiteness within education are hegemonic and omnipresent.

Epistemological Subcontract

Whiteness is able to reconcile for itself something that it forbids for other groups... whites may be irrational and claim reason at the very same time. They can represent two irreconcilable positions; the one of ignorance and the other of knowledge. Whites would not tolerate this for others (Leonardo, p. 93)

The epistemological subcontract, another tentacle of the Racial Contract, pays close attention to how individuals and society both understand, interpret, and misinterpret the Racial Contract. Definitionally, epistemology is how one comes to make sense of meanings, words, phrases, and ideas and how one comes to know what they know and why. Within the context of the Racial Contract, the epistemological contract is how to make sense of the Contract through a frame or lens of whiteness. Because so much of the Contract relies on upholding hegemonic whiteness, it is often in the best interest of whites to not only misinterpret it but to actively be blind to it. In as much, Leonardo discusses a philosophy of white epistemological discourse, which is a set of skills that white people use so that they know when, how, where, and with whom to participate in racial discourse. This functions so that whites can maintain a sense of equilibrium whilst upholding white dominance. White people can stay and interact with others so that their sense of the world is not disrupted and challenged. As just one example, Smith, Funaki, and MacDonald

(2021) argue that the white university can remain hegemonically white even when discussing issues of racial inclusion and equity. White discourse is quite versatile in proclaiming to work towards policies of equity and inclusion insofar as these policies do not disrupt the whiteness of the university.

The Racial Contract is also "grounded in an epistemology that lacks consistency and defies logic but does not produce cognitive dissonance because it remains consistent with the Racial Contract" (Leonardo, p.92). It relies on an overt engagement and expression of gymnastic-like thinking so as to avoid any sense that whites are participating in racist or discriminatory behaviour. Within this perspective, whites not only misunderstand their own image and creation, they do not know what they have done nor do they need to know. Thus, when the logic of an argument and way of understanding the world becomes part of the fabric of society, the ability to challenge it becomes even more difficult. This is quite clear when white university students are given an education that is congruent with their educational upbringing, personal and societal experiences, as well as self-knowledge. Education from a white lens and framework speaks to how and in what capacity a topic or scholar is deemed either 'inside' or 'outside' the canon. The epistemological subcontract relies on whiteness being at the centre of all knowledge that is deemed worthy, whilst everything else is framed in juxtaposition or as an 'other' or alternative perspective.

The epistemological subcontract also upholds willful critical blindness (Morrison,1992) and an epistemology of white ignorance[4] (Mills, Applebaum). Leonardo posits that willful critical blindness cannot effectively be upheld through any type of rationality. It requires an incoherence that must be part of whites' personal and collective development. Awatare (1984) builds on this, noting how white people create and maintain a blissful state of grace where such ignorance is valued as innocence. She deploys the metaphor of a sign outside of a kindergarten classroom. This sign states, 'Māori keep out. For white use only.' White people cannot see the sign. As per the Contract, one must identify as Māori (internalising a minoritised and status of the 'O'ther) in order to see and understand it. If whites were to expose the truth of the Contract, their sense of self and view of the social world could be uprooted, and their status of white domination would be under threat.

However, when whiteness is interrogated, the binary that often frames conversations about race (i.e., racist/not-racist) as it connects to a framework

---

[4] An epistemology of white ignorance will be discussed in detail in chapter 4.

or web of whiteness becomes more nuanced. Mills (1997) argues for an understanding of the cognitive processes that typically produce false beliefs. He states, "the aim is to understand how certain social structures tend to promote these crucially flawed processes, how to personally extricate oneself from them, and to do one's part in undermining them in the broader cognitive sphere" (p.23). Within this context, students and educators have the potential to begin to question seemingly benign philosophies and practices that are often framed as colour-blind and merit-based. By looking to, and challenging the epistemological subcontract, therein lies the possibility of exposing the structuring effects of racial privilege for white thinking.

Whiteness as Bully

The concept of whiteness as bully, as it is situated and contextualised within the Racial Contract, intersects with the social construction of race and whiteness and its relationship to power, privilege and status. Racial categories have been invented and reinvented, as various groups have been denied, assigned, and reassigned the status of whiteness over and across time. The social construction of whiteness underpins power, privilege, and hierarchy. The ideas of racial construction and formation, racial reconstruction, and the assignment of whiteness have shifted over time and are geographically, politically, and historically contextualised. What has always been consistent, however, is that solidarity with whiteness and one's proximity to whiteness too often trumps solidarity based on class, gender, and sexuality, among others.

Whiteness as bully speaks to why whites have, sometimes unwittingly, signed onto the Contract as a way to cope with their own social injuries, such as class exploitation and patriarchy. Leonardo articulates this well:

> Like other bullies, whiteness exacts its price, mainly by exerting its social pressure for denigrated whites to stay in line and abide by their loyalties to the white race and its quest for domination... they carry out the terrorism of whiteness at the same time they are terrorized by it (p.95).

Wilkerson (2020), author of *Caste*, further explains and reinforces that slavery was created by and for the benefits of the white elite and enforced by the poorest white members of society. The result of this was the maintenance of solidarity in one's whiteness rather than their economic status. This perspective reinforces various forms of oppression that uphold an us vs. them mentality. Wilkerson understands the malaise of insecurities as a dominant group status threat. In the United States, the least well-off, most precariously situated members of the dominant group for many years took for granted their status and hierarchy and the benefits that came with it. This precarity comes with resentment, which could be heard through the 'take our country back' mantra of 2016, 2020, and now again, in 2024. Whiteness as bully manifests through the politics of nativism, patriotism, populism, and Make America Great Again (MAGA). Whiteness as bully requires that Black, Indigenous, and People of Colour become the object of torment. This actually reinforces the power of whiteness in its overt juxtaposition to blackness. '*People are voting against their own best interests...*' This is a commonly used phrase that attempts to explain those who voted for Trump. In reality, whites who support Trump are actually voting on behalf of their whiteness, as they vote with and for whites. In other words, the dominant status group may lose everything, but they will not lose their whiteness.

Rewriting the Contract

Significantly, when there is an awareness of the Racial Contract and its interconnecting subcontracts, therein lies the possibility and potential to rewrite and sign off on it. Like hegemony, rupturing the Contract holds out possibilities for disconsenting. Leonardo (2015) believes that white investment is pedagogical, arguing that the extent to which racial supremacy is taught to white students, it can be 'untaught' or 'unlearnt.' Insofar as it is pedagogical, there is the possibility of critically reflecting on its flaws to disrupt it. White teachers and white students have the potential to challenge themselves (and others) to radically question the Racial Contract by breaking an oath of loyalty to whiteness. Educators and students must think about, interrogate, and unsettle such content within their university learning communities so that they can move about the world differently, whilst considering the interconnected systems of oppression and how they are upheld within the white university. Thus, white educators and their students become an integral component of the protestation of educational regimes and institutions that create and maintain whiteness and white domination.

This point is further articulated by Tuhiwai Smith (1999), who discusses the need for histories to be retold, authenticated, and rewritten to interrogate the oppression of theories that continue to be perpetuated and unchallenged within the academy. Denzin and Lincoln (2008) further argue that because of the status quo of dominant epistemologies of western knowledge production, such ways of thinking about and questioning education are deemed irrelevant in academia. Within Aotearoa, New Zealand, there have been many forms of radical resistance to the Contract. An intellectual movement called Kaupapa Māori[5] continues to advocate for creating epistemological and intellectual spaces that combine an analysis of the structural conditions of colonisation with political mobilisation (Kidman et al., 2018). Falling in line with Freire's notion of educating for critical consciousness and self-reflexivity as they relate to critical learning and action, Kaupapa Māori is geared towards social change and educational transformation.

Leonardo also sees the process of rewriting the contract as becoming an epistemological traitor. If understanding that epistemology is how one comes to make sense of the world, then working towards becoming an epistemological traitor is moving towards a space that unpacks hegemonic and structural whiteness whilst unlearning and relearning to activate a critical racial consciousness. Whites must radically question the Racial Contract and its subcontracts. It is an essential process when working towards epistemic justice and disrupting systemic ignorance. As an ideology of whiteness is part of a hermeneutics of the self rather than a biological destiny, various identities are, in fact, a hybrid of how one might understand themself. In as much, with whiteness emerging as an authentic worldview, it becomes imperative to understand that white racism is inherently oppressive, but whiteness seen through the prism of reconstructionism is multifaceted and undecidable (Leonardo, 2009). Thus, working towards the development of critical consciousness involves educating to challenge systems of power, privilege, and oppression, all of which can contribute to social change. The next section looks at the concept of Historical Privilege, another philosophy that has the potential to challenge, unsettle and interrogate the white university.

Historical Privilege

Historical privilege situates historical and contemporary power and their relationship to sustained generational white supremacy. The idea of historical privilege (Borrel et al.,2018) explains how opportunities for some (privilege and power) result in marginalisation and fewer opportunities (trauma) for others. Historical privilege is cumulative and sustained through a whitewashing and one-sided account of history. Again, I draw on Awatare (1984), who argues this point well as it relates to the history of colonisation in Aotearoa, New Zealand.

---

[5] Kaupapa Māori means Māori principles, philosophies, practices and values. Within this context it refers to political and social movements (Kidman et. al. 2018).

Awatare argues that Māori were forced to accept the white will over their own, and to acquiesce to the power of white sovereignty. Māori were forced to live by rules not of their own making. She states, "these rules condemned us to a defeated life. The destiny of the Māori people was altered" (p.14). The result of a whitewashed account of the historical and ongoing practices of colonisation is how white people live lives that are dominated by permanent amnesia. "Amnesia allows white people to forget that their current occupation and 'ownership' of our country rests on the fact of forceful alienation of our country of our tipuna (ancestors)" (Awatare, 1984, p.66). The result of this is a permanent forgetfulness, and a laundered history and denial of reciprocity for the deeds of one's ancestors. Amnesia is vital for the well-being of white people.

Similarly, Kinchole (1999) adds that the history of the world's diverse peoples, as well as minoritised groups in western societies has been told from a white historiographical perspective. Within this narrative, the manner that history is told, remembered, and misremembered reinforces the need to pay attention to a deliberate omission of a true account of history. As Goldberg (2009) states, While the politics of colonial history involve moving on, getting over, and forgetting the past, anti-racist politics "requires historical memory, recalling the conditions of racial degradation and relating contemporary to historical and local to global conditions" (Goldberg, 2009, p.21 as cited within McConville et al., 2019).

Historical privilege specifically speaks to the complex system of collective structural advantages that are experienced over time and across generations by a group of people who share an identity, affiliation, or circumstance. As just one example from the United States, post-reconstruction era policies in North Carolina forbade formerly enslaved Black people to trade or sell goods of any kind. If they were caught doing so, they would be subjected to severe physical punishment. Consequently, this blocked any means to earn money from their own farm labors and forced them into economic dependence on the white elite. Thus, what used to be de jure policies and laws morphed into de facto practices that kept Black people from moving up the economic ladder, or really, any avenue for economic improvement or social mobility. Wilkerson (2020) captures this well within the following statement:

> The historic association between menial labor and blackness served to further entrap black people in a circle of subservience in the American mind. They were punished for being in the conditions that they were forced to endure. And the image of servitude shadowed them into freedom (p.135)

Such philosophies and practices shifted and morphed over time, reinforcing systems and polices that further uphold educational, occupational, and financial hierarchies. The spillover and cumulative effect of these policies seep into all aspects of society. White people benefit from the deeds of others of their culture in cyclic time, the generations before. Without an understanding of colonial history and group position, discourses of equal opportunity and meritocracy become a justification for undermining group-based social services and affirmative action, as it is assumed that all structural impediments to an equitable society have been addressed McConville et al. (2019). With this argument, 'success' becomes synonymous with hard work, individual achievement, and strong work ethic rather than a historical context of racism and dispossession, i.e., neoliberal racism[6]. This is also seen in Aotearoa, New Zealand. After Pākehā soldiers returned from overseas after the war, they were 'gifted' stolen Māori land. This 'gift' for serving in the army came at the expense of land confiscation and colonisation (Jackson, 2016).

Fittingly, inheritance (cognitive/non-cognitive skills, educational achievement, etc.) are taken as a given in that 'successes' and 'failures' are often individualised rather than seen as a product of historical and generational privileges. These two points reinforce what Jackson (2016) refers to as the 'mythtakes' of history, which include the prioritising of master narratives whilst engaging in a form of active forgetting. Echoing this, Kidman et al. (2019) note:

> The ways that different groups remember and forget the difficult or violent histories that sit beneath official 'birth of the nation' stories also influence what is taught in schools… a rewriting and reorganising of colonial violence whereby acts of brutality and invasion are transformed into patriotic tales of settler and pioneer heroism which then seep into the curricula and pedagogical practice of education (235).

Hegemonic interpretations relegate colonisation to the past; a single moment of relative insignificance (McConville et al.). Through such masked and insidious rhetoric, a society that is built upon foundations of racism, colonialism, and white supremacy, the cumulative advantages for the dominant racial and/or ethnic group are often seamlessly concealed and justified. The subversive nature of such justification requires a deep analysis of what might be going on within educational communities (in this context, the university), recognising that education and society are one and the same. However, it is incomplete to start a

---

[6] Neoliberal racism will be discussed in more depth in chapter 4.

discussion of whiteness, racism, and educational exclusion at the university level. Instead, there must be an awareness of how deeply rooted, systemic, and predetermined education is from the very start. The pipeline of education has been set up from the beginning to exclude and dominate through a white lens and framework. What follows is a broad overview of the education debt and its sub-debts: *historical, economic, socio-political, and moral* (Ladson-Billings, 2006), as well as a brief discussion of their interconnectivity to the Racial Contract and Historical Privilege. Ultimately, all three philosophies reinforce how concurrently they work in tandem to uphold whiteness and racial domination within and beyond education.

The Education Debt

Education, at all levels, is framed and often esteemed as something that has the potential to challenge social inequities and multiple forms of marginalisation. However, and somewhat ironically, education not only fails to address these issues institutionally, but this failure also reinforces and often upholds said inequalities outside of education. Recognising the interconnecting relationship between education and society, this final section speaks to Anyon's (2011) argument that education and society are inextricably linked, in that both rely on one another to contribute to the reproduction and hegemony of social classes, the economy, and racial and gender exclusion and subordination. To further develop this idea, I draw on critical education scholar Gloria Ladson-Billings (2006) and her conceptual understanding of the education debt.

Ladson-Billings (2006) argues that education is framed and discussed the wrong way. Instead of understanding educational achievement as one-dimensional and static, there must be a reworking of interpretations that note an abundance or scarcity of *opportunities* in education, tracing these ideas throughout history up until the present. Ladson-Billings argues that the 'achievement gap' has been studied *ed nauseum* and argues that there is no achievement gap, but rather, there is an education debt. Ladson-Billings pays attention to various education debts (historical, economic, socio-political, and moral), outlining how they work in tandem to suppress opportunities in education, as well as perpetuate and systematise racism, stratification, and marginalisation. Ladson-Billings' analysis further speaks to and reinforces the pipeline and matrix of educational inequity; beginning from primary/elementary, all the way through university education.

To understand the nuances that underpin the challenges within educational communities, it is helpful to tease apart the differences between equity and equality, as they are often used interchangeably, but are, in fact, quite different.

Equality is the belief that the playing field is levelled and that if one tries their hardest, they can achieve anything. If not, it is the fault of the individual. Conversely, equity is the understanding and recognition that not everyone starts at the same place nor has the same opportunities (educational, financial, access, etc.). In fact, there is no base or common denominator that can be used as a starting point, as everyone comes to the table with different experiences.

In fact, students, teachers, and communities often believe that 'failure' is the result of individual action and lack of motivation rather than the consideration of societal, institutional, and exclusionary practices; again, speaking to an institutionalisation of oppression and inferiority. Lipman (2016) recognises this as a "process that works its way into the discourses and practices of schools, through the actions of not only elites, but also marginalised and oppressed people acting in conditions, not of their own making" (p. 121). Therefore, when engaging in conversations about education, the underlying premise is that there are many and diverse circumstances that lead to educational disparities and pronounced inequities within education. I further develop and analyse these circumstances through Ladson-Billings' framework of an Education Debt: Historical, Economic, Sociopolitical, and Moral.

Historical Debt

The historical debt (which, in many ways, is an extension of historical privilege) explains the long-standing and persistent way that education operates in an inequitable and oppressive manner. DiAngelo (2012) argues that by removing the historical dimensions from analysis, it is harder to develop a nuanced understanding of all that has occurred in the past and denies that everyone is a product of a historical lineage. This denial also prevents an understanding of how the past bears upon the present and how it has led to the current conditions in which one finds oneself. Within the context of the United States, education and society have been inextricably connected to one other since the birth of public schools (Anyon, 2005 & 2011; Ayers and Ayers, 2011, Labaree, 1997; Lipman, 2011, Spring, 1988 & 1996; Tyack, 2003). One of the salient links between the two has historically been, and continues to be, the role schools and education play in working to mould the *ideal American,* or what Hinchey (2008) describes as " a process intended to blend the individuals into one mass, and eventually producing a homogenous standard product" (p. 8). Schooling was founded on a colonial and white interpretation of what counts as education, who should access it, and what its purposes really are. The historical debt demonstrates that education has always been experienced in a way that reinforces hegemonic whiteness, exclusion, racial domination, and marginalisation.

The historical debt recognises that education was forbidden for many students and families of colour since the beginning of public education. It is not an accident that education has never been equitable and accessible. A few of the most egregious and concrete ways that education is/was not only segregated but deliberately oppressive for many groups in the United States can be seen within the following examples: Freedmen's schools (enslaved African Americans were prohibited from schooling) English-only teaching with Native American and Latinx children (among others), separate and unequal hand-me-down textbooks, shorter school year for rural Black students, missionary schools (which used American Indian labour to further the cause of the church) and, American Indian boarding schools, 'Kill the Indian, save the man.' Within the context of Aotearoa, New Zealand, a system of state-run Native elementary schools was introduced in 1867. Today, students are still subjected to colonial education, whitewashing Māori history, undermining colonisation, (both past and present) as well as punishing students who speak te reo Māori. [7] These examples are clearly not exhaustive but rather offer a few concrete ways to understand how racial domination and whiteness have historically (and currently to be) privileged within education, access, and achievement.

Economic Debt

The economic debt sits alongside the historical debt and is paramount to a discussion and analysis of education today. Funding disparities between high and low socioeconomic schools tell a story about the value placed on the education of poor, Black, Indigenous and Students of Color and their white counterparts. Rooks (as cited in Strauss, V. 2018) elaborates on this argument through a term she calls *segrenomics*. Rooks focuses her analysis on segregation, educational inequity in the United States, and the ways that many current reforms and policies not only reinforce different types of education between poor and wealthy students, but how said policies uphold capitalism and wealth accumulation. She states, "if we as a nation really took seriously dismantling underperforming school districts and replacing them with the same types of educational experiences we provide the wealthy, it would negatively impact the bottom line of many companies" (Strauss, 2018). Throughout her analysis, Rooks intersects the goals of neoliberalism with

---

[7] Te reo Māori is the Indigenous language of Māori in Aotearoa New Zealand.

demeaning, dehumanising, and self-responsibilisation in education. She reinforces how interconnected these three facets are to the sustainability of wealth and capital. Relatedly, Picower and Mayorga (2016) remind us,

> While wealth and power accrue, the language of individual responsibility for solving social problems and meritocracy turn a blind eye to those historical inequities… the rhetoric of reform and justice is woven into the values of the market and becomes a veil for the protection of capitalist accumulation (p.9).

Rooks, Picower, and Mayorga's argument exposes and highlights the often taken-for-granted interconnectivity between history, politics, education and society, whilst paying close attention to the fact that one cannot be attended to without the other. Once again, failure is perceived as an individual problem as opposed to something that is societal or systemic. Schools create educational channels that efficiently carry groups of students toward different locations in the occupational structure. Within this framework, schools become the most important vehicle to prepare children to be 'productive' members of society. Likewise, this model breeds further inequity in that the better one 'achieves' in school, the more possibilities become available for higher education and better jobs, etc.

Whiteness as bully and the economic debt are also mutually inclusive and have political and social repercussions. In his book *Broke and Patriotic*, Dunia (2018) traversed the United States by interviewing those who live in the lowest socioeconomic communities. Throughout his research, Dunia argues that the poor (regardless of racial background or ethnic identification) are the most patriotic of Americans. On the surface, this might seem like a walking contradiction. However, what Dunia paid close attention to is the individual blame that many poor Americans place on BIPOC communities, immigrants, and 'radical liberals,' as well as privileging and equating whiteness and proximity to whiteness as being a 'true American.' Dunia discusses how many poor Americans feel angry about the country moving away from its religious foundations, ideologies of 'meritocracy and success,' as well as the premise that diversity and identity politics are the true demise of a country. Such framing consumes a white supremacist ideology, institutionalised forms of oppression, as well as couched language that places blame upon Black, Indigenous, and People of Colour, reinforcing an 'us' vs 'them' mentality.

Sociopolitical Debt

The sociopolitical debt is arguably the most insidious and often the hardest to see directly. The markers of this debt manifest and become so institutionalised that they tend to be explained away through colour-blind ideologies and hegemonic interpretations of racism, sexism, and classism. Offering a few examples from primary and secondary education, the sociopolitical debt includes the exclusion of Black, Indigenous, and Families of Colour from policy and decision-making, the make-up of school board representation, Parent Teacher Association groups, school boards, fundraising, school site council, etc. Often excused or explained away as a lack of interest from those who are not involved (rather than external factors that often exclude and/or make participating difficult), the sociopolitical debt reinforces that nothing is accidental nor happenstance. The education system is set up so that whiteness and a white lens and perspective are the norm for philosophies, policies, decision-making, etc. Education that privileges a white framework upholds positions of power, how schools are run, and reinforces inequitable learning opportunities and experiences. All these factors contribute to understanding the ramifications of the sociopolitical debt and its relationship to education.

Another example that further emphasises the long-lasting implications of the sociopolitical debt is through curriculum making and the adoption of teaching and learning national standards in the United States. The Texas State Board of Education is often tasked with creating and making decisions on the standards that students are expected to learn throughout their formative years of schooling. Texas has historically been a more conservative state that often elects white, religious, and right-wing board members to committees such as the state board of education. As a result, teaching and learning become co-opted by those who do not see the relevance of culturally responsive teaching, as well as those who advocate for curriculum decisions that whitewash United States history (Muñoz & Noboa, 2018). In the US, there are currently policies and movements to ban books, as well as a rise in physical and verbal attacks on those who teach critical race theory[8] and sexuality education in schools. Within the Aotearoa context, the new government coalition (National, ACT and New Zealand First) are working to dismantle the Labour-led (2017-2023)

---

[8] The battle over bringing critical race theory (CRT) into classrooms is framed as another element of identity politics and free speech. Opponents of CRT see it as including divisive topics, as well as creating division between groups based on their race, gender, sexuality, etc. Critical race theory will be more fully discussed in chapter 5.

introduction of Aotearoa-based history curriculum, entitled, Te Takanga o Te Wā in *Te Marautanga o Aotearoa* and Aotearoa New Zealand's histories (education.gov.nz, 2024) This new curriculum foregrounds the teaching of history in Aotearoa New Zealand through a critical lens and framework. Seen as a threat to teaching students the historical and current impact of colonisation and settler colonialism, as well as worrying about white students feeling guilty, the rolling back of critical teaching of history reinforces a carefully crafted system of education that prioritises whiteness, standardisation and its seeming neutrality. This decision-making reinforces the power of content and curricular choices, in this case, directly leaving out the voices of marginalised communities, particularly those that expose and challenge, institutional and racialised structures and experiences. These policies and narratives have lasting repercussions for whose histories are told, which knowledges are disseminated as 'T'ruth, as well as the ways students come to see and understand themselves as racialised beings within their own educational experiences.

The sociopolitical debt also extends to university education. As a result of the neoliberal university, it should not come as a surprise that too many university courses fail to move beyond and challenge the western canon of learning and knowledge production (Tuhiwai Smith, 1999). Neoliberalism and neoconservatism often work in tandem, prioritising the free market, competition, and individualism, whilst simultaneously pushing back on radical voices from the margins (cultural, racialised, economic, gendered, and sexual borderlands) that challenge such ideologies. Quite subversively, within the university, there is a reconstruction of indigenous-settler epistemic relationships in ways that seem to affirm colonial forms of knowledge production while simultaneously adhering to neoliberal, economic and ideological imperatives (Kidman, 2019). Thus, within the neoliberal classroom, any pedagogy that asks professors and students to critically self-reflect and confront their own biases as they relate to race, is increasingly threatened by the institutional support for courses that focus on 'technical' knowledge that prepares students for marketable job skills (Fillion Wilson, 2019).

Notably, this debt speaks to the insidious ways that educational, societal, and structural oppressions manifest. Success and failure (in this case, within the university) are seen as individual and the fault of one's own doing, as opposed to recognising how a culture of omnipresent racism, sexism, and white supremacy reinforces such binary thinking. The historical, economic, and sociopolitical debts demonstrate how education systematically and institutionally marginalises too many students, and communities. However, even after considering and unpacking these three debts (and like rewriting the Racial Contract), Ladson-Billings envisions a hopeful future through an understanding of the moral debt.

Moral Debt

The moral debt directly challenges the historical, economic, and sociopolitical debts. It also coincides with the potential to collectively sign off the Racial Contact. Ladson-Billings argues that the moral debt creates opportunities to reimagine inequitable and oppressive education. If considered within the framework of understanding power and interconnectivity, the moral debt helps to explain how and why the education debt upholds whiteness and inequity both within education and society.

Engaging the moral debt, Ladson-Billings looks to Saint Thomas Aquinas (1225-1274), who saw the moral debt as what human beings owe each other in the giving of, or failure to give, one another. Aquinas pointed to the importance of honouring when honour is due. In other words, how might one move into a space where there becomes a deliberate attempt to do what one knows is right (Aquinas, as cited within Ladson-Billings, 2006)? How does one couple personal responsibility with social responsibility? Most important, what is it that one owes to members of their communities who have historically and currently continue to be excluded from social benefits and opportunities? The moral debt presents an opportunity to move away from surface-level approaches to address multiple forms of marginalisation, racial domination, and whiteness as an ideology. Significantly, there must be an engagement with a more nuanced and deliberate approach to interrogating whiteness when considering the ramifications of the debts, and, by extension, signing off the Contract.

Conclusion

When considering the potential to undermine the problem of the 'white university', it is vital to embrace a multitude of cognitive perspectives by developing the practice of self-reflexivity and educating for critical consciousness. This coincides with Greene (1998), who argues that a praxis of educational consequence opens the spaces necessary for the remaking of a democratic society. This kind of society provides a space where the unconditional freedom to question and assert one's voice, however different, is central to the purpose of education and democracy. Signing off the Contract and engaging with the moral debt are active and purposeful processes, just like the characteristics of democracy and freedom. They must be conceptualised as dialogical and dialectical, understanding educators and students as agents of social change and transformation. There must be a commitment to challenging assumptions and reexamining fundamental principles without guarantees, but with an expanded sense of hope, confidence, and possibility (Ayers and Ayers, 2011).

Behind the shield that upholds the walls of whiteness within the university, it is too easy to either centre whiteness or focus on the invisibility of its privilege and power in a very surfaced manner. Through a multi-faceted discussion of the Racial Contract, Historical Privilege, and Education Debt, this chapter discussed how, philosophically, the historical, political, social, and economic components of education work in tandem to reinforce how whiteness exists and manifests within the university. I now move to a discussion of two specific concepts and practices that uphold and maintain the white university: *diversity* and *colour blindness*. Engaging the second prong within the three-pronged approach, the following chapter speaks directly to how the 'problem' of the white university is upheld and reproduced. To move even deeper with the discussion of the white university, I analyse how diversity and colour-blindness maintain and sustain whiteness through language, policies, and behaviours.

Chapter 4

Diversity and Colour-blindness (Three-pronged approach question 2- How is the 'problem' upheld and maintained?)

Introduction

Chapter three discussed the 'problem' of the white university, theorising it through the Racial Contract, Historical Privilege, and Education Debt. My intention throughout the previous chapter was to zoom out in a way that presents the problem of the white university like a forest, an interconnected system that has many moving and intersecting components (trees, shrubs, animals, etc.). All the members of the forest (and within this metaphor, the forest is the university) know their roles in order to uphold the system as it presently works and exists. Of significance, many members of the forest (and the university) community don't question the way it works, or that there might be a problem with the current system. This is the essence of the first prong, which discusses the 'problem,' often to the surprise of the members involved. The white university is comprised of a variety of people, policies, philosophies, etc., who work in tandem, and rely upon one another (even without knowing they are doing so) to keep the university just as it should be; in-tact and thriving through privileging whiteness and upholding racial domination.

The purpose of chapter four is to highlight and discuss that the 'problem' of the white university is, in fact, a problem. With the structural and philosophical intricacies of the white university exposed throughout the previous chapter, I move to the second prong and take a deep dive into some of the behaviours and practices that uphold and maintain the white university. Throughout this chapter, I analyse the ideologies, language, and philosophies that reinforce the whiteness of the university. Specifically, I focus on *diversity* and *colour-blindness*, discussing what they are and how they uphold whiteness, particularly within the university context. First, I untangle the term diversity, discussing how it is deployed to maintain and protect systems and spaces of whiteness. I look to the ideas *desiring diversity* (Patel, 2015) and *diversity regimes* (Thomas, 2018) as both demonstrate how, without understanding the subversiveness behind the terms, they often do more harm than the good intentions they purport to embody.

Next, I unpack colour-blindness and engage it through three specific concepts and ideas: *hegemonic whiteness, an epistemology of ignorance, and neoliberal racism.* I demonstrate how all three concepts work together to uphold and perpetuate colour-blindness within all aspects of the university culture, both behaviorally and philosophically. Although the meanings of diversity and colour-blindness have shifted over time, their purposes and ideologies reinforce the social construction of race, hegemonic whiteness, and neoliberal racism. The purpose of untangling terms like diversity and colour-blindness is to provide a language that helps explain *why* and *how* the white university continues to exist and remain in-tact. As is the case with nebulous understandings of terminology like race and whiteness, there must be an interrogation of taken-for-granted concepts and ideas, as by not knowing what or why something is being challenged, it is difficult to interrupt and work to transform it.

Presently, the current global rhetoric within and around university campuses (generally speaking) is that there seems to be an awareness that action must be taken to address racism and whiteness in academia. However, this talk is merely symbolic if there isn't a deeper understanding of *how* the current language regarding such action within the university is deployed. If such language remains uninterrogated, the walls of whiteness are sustained, making them stronger and higher. The reality and contradiction within universities is that they seemingly desire to challenge racism, believe they judge one another through individuality and objectivity, whilst simultaneously recognising that they need to 'diversify' academia. Additionally, university strategies promise to remove barriers to access for underrepresented groups and develop learning spaces that are free from racism and discrimination, etc. However, as Hoskins & Jones (2023) argue in response to the Tertiary Education Commission's strategy for universities in Aotearoa, New Zealand, these are admirable priorities that dominate educational rhetoric. However, they lack any philosophical and political framework for genuine change. These policies argue that things need to change, but the reality is that nothing does nor will actually change.

Diversity and colour-blindness, seemingly contradictory terms, rely upon each other to subversively maintain the white university. Colour-blindness, as an ideology, is often deployed in 'race-neutral' spaces, which insidiously works to uphold structures, policies and philosophies that cater to keeping the university hegemonically white. Diversity, on the other hand, when used as a descriptor or tool for addressing or confronting racism, tends to be symbolic. Institutions of higher education more often reflect a *desire* for the appearance of diversity, instead of working towards interrogating and challenging pervasive structural and racial inequalities that actually undermine genuine change. Colour-blindness and diversity serve as euphemisms for feel-good rhetoric about the thought of working to transform the university to be more socially just (another overused term). They allow the philosophies and practices of everyday whiteness to seep into all sectors of the university, upholding the same structures they claim to challenge.

Ahmed (2012) articulates this point well through the following statement (italics added): University strategies for diversity become about *changing perceptions of whiteness rather than changing the whiteness of organisations.* Changing perceptions rather than practices and policies of whiteness is how an institution continues to reproduce it. This purposefully confusing rhetoric of whiteness sits within the same space and interpretation as the social construction of race. Just as who is defined as white has shifted across time, history, and geography (Jacobson, 1998) so too has the concept of the social construction of race. Mills (1997, 2007) discusses the seemingly 'benign' question of asking someone 'what are you?' or 'where are you *really* from' (italics added)? What these questions actually provide the asker is, 'where are you located on the racial hierarchy and/or racial continuum?' Once this placement has been situated and 'understood', the asker can then deploy preconceived notions and biases that uphold stereotypes and stereotype threat[1] (Steele, 1997). Racial categorisation becomes an invisible guide not only in terms of how one speaks and acts, but also in regard to the way information is processed. By categorising someone within a racial hierarchy, as well as on a continuum of racial identification, it becomes easier to locate their proximity and/or distance from and to whiteness. However, although race is socially constructed (rather than biological), the ramifications and consequences of one's racial location are real. What follows is a discussion of the concept of diversity, demonstrating how it is used as a distraction and/or cover-up when attempting to discuss race and whiteness within university and education contexts.

---

[1] Stereotype is being at risk of confirming, supporting, or upholding a negative stereotype about one's group.

Diversity

By using diversity as a proxy for nonwhite, and not being explicit about the structures and histories that privilege whiteness, institutions of higher education have implicitly left unchallenged the racially stratified nature of society and how that echoes and is maintained on college campuses (Patel, 2015).

With the current political climate on university campuses, the discussion of 'diversity and inclusion[2]' has become ubiquitous, or as Thomas (2018) terms it, 'ubiquitous emptiness'. It is no longer acceptable (in progressive circles, at least) to deny the existence of structural racism and the need to acknowledge the problematic ways that universities uphold whiteness and white supremacy. The term diversity is used within university mission statements, faculty hiring job ads, student retention, language, course syllabi, and even course titles. Diversity is often deployed as a technique for rearranging things so organisations can appear in a better or 'happier' way. Ambikaipaker (2019) correctly argues, "hierarchical institutions routinely place inclusion and equality as subordinate priorities in relation to other values, goals, and projects" (p.268). Further, Ovink & Murrell (2022) discuss how the phrase 'cosmetic diversity' is used to describe universities that give the appearance of ethnoracial diversity, but such appearances tend to be more performative. A recent survey on racism in Aotearoa New Zealand universities by the Te Hautū Kahurangi |Tertiary Education Union demonstrates cosmetic diversity in practice. A survey participant noted:

We have taken a hollow ritualistic approach to cultural issues. Lots of nice emails with Māori greetings, but no real cultural changes to a more participative and collectivist way of running the university. The language stuff is easy, but the culture change stuff is much harder (2024).

---

[2] DEI (Diversity, Equity, and Inclusion) programs and roles on university campuses in the United States are experiencing a very contentious moment. There is little understanding for the *how* and *why* DEI programs are needed to address the historical and current ways that universities have and continue to reinforce racial domination and whiteness. Elements of this chapter should resonate with the larger discussion that undergirds the controversy of DEI programs and policies. See https://truthout.org/articles/amid-extremist-attacks-on-higher-ed-we-must-go-beyond-diversity-and-inclusion/ for further reading.

Significantly, by peppering tokenistic cultural practices and some language inclusion, campuses may appear to be making changes, but in reality, they continue to remain hegemonically white spaces. Within this perspective, diversity is like institutional polishing; it is shiny but underneath it is rotten.

Diversity is also framed as something that should be tolerated and celebrated. Circling back to Lorde and her discussion of tolerance, there is nothing inherently proactive or radical about tolerating someone. When being tolerant of difference or diversity, there is the assumption that this 'other' must be celebrated and applauded. Furthermore, engaging in sentiments of 'being tolerant' echoes feelings of false collaboration and inauthenticity. Similarly, the term diversity is nebulous enough to sound proactive and transformative, but it often serves as a placeholder for self-congratulatory representation. Highlighting this point, Eddo-Lodge argues, "my blackness has been politicised against my will, but I don't want it wilfully ignored in an effort to instil some sort of precarious, false harmony" (p. 82, 2017). I would be hard pressed to find educational institutions that are not concerned with their status and reputation, as well as those who state that their university strategic plan includes having a more diverse student body and inclusive academic community. However, careful attention must be paid to why, how, and in what capacity institutions of higher education strive and discuss the term diversity.

Thus, I ask, how is the term diversity deployed, and who 'counts' as being diverse? I remember when I was a primary educator and a white staff member commented how 'diverse' our student population was. The make- up of the school was 99% Black/African American. Thus, the student body was not diverse when taking in to account the racial representation of our school and student population. What this statement demonstrated was that 'diverse,' as understood by the white teacher, referred to the racial makeup of the school in comparison to the greater racial makeup of the city writ large. Through this teacher's understanding of race, diversity meant not-white, which was the majority of the school, but was not representative of the community outside of the school. In other words, compared to the whiteness of the community, the 'not-white' student body was deemed 'diverse.' This example illustrates why it is important to pay close attention to the manner in which diversity is conceptualised, the meanings behind seemingly benign words, and the ways that people and communities are categorised and racialised.

Building on this argument, the reality of how the university aims to be 'diverse' and 'inclusive' can also be challenged in communal spaces on campus. In their ethnographic study of settler (white) norms at a university in Aotearoa,

New Zealand, Smith, Funaki, and MacDonald (2021) found that within the common space at their respective university, white and settler norms are upheld, even though this space purports to be 'inclusive.' In fact, the whiteness of the space was upheld by who was and who was not present. Smith et al. state,

> When we entered the [communal space] we noticed immediately that it was largely inhabited by white students...if Māori or Pacific were the predominant group of people here, it would be out of the ordinary. People would wonder if there was a special event going on-its use by non-dominant groups would need to be explained (p.138).

The normativity of communal spaces as being designed for white comfort reinforces the way diversity is framed within many university campuses that claim inclusivity means 'for everyone.' In reality, such communal spaces are designed so that white people feel comfortable and at home in all places (consider the spatial subcontract of the Racial Contract). These spaces normalise whiteness. Conversely, the availability of areas designed for BIPOC (non-settler) groups and the design of the communal space contribute to the unspoken agreement that whites can and do belong everywhere.

The *thought* of diversifying the university also sits within the same feel-good rhetoric that characterises the 'good white.' As Thomas (2018) argues, diversity is 'happy talk,' as it allows one to be blind to the structural issues of race and inequality. Universities can't claim they are racist if they are working hard to diversify their campuses, i.e., making them 'less white.' Thus, diversity is framed as something tangible that can be done (doing diversity) so that institutions can engage in a series of checkboxes that accomplish a single goal of increased racial representation (not-white). In fact, Thomas notes, "as multiple signifiers of diversity are brought into meaningful relationships with one another to articulate diversity, diversity is made to be everywhere and nowhere at the same time" (p. 147, 2018). Since diversity is often framed as an add-on, it can be seen as benign and self-congratulatory as opposed to something that will aid in the disruption of the status quo of whiteness. Even the term diversity appears less threatening, but it is also doing less because it does not really mean anything. Bringing in 'diversity' is often interconnected with assuaging feelings of white guilt. By including Black, Indigenous and People of Colour (even cosmetically), the whiteness of the institution seems to be temporarily suspended with feel-good rhetoric of 'doing something.'

Thus, at present, the term and concept of diversity become not only trite, but it is also meaningless and opaque. Contemporary initiatives for diversity reflect a desire for the appearance of diversity without unsettling or challenging the pervasiveness of structural and institutional inequality. As McAllister et al. (2019) argue, the policies of benevolent inclusion for a range of marginalised or underrepresented groups appear to fall well short of the goals and principles they publicly support and endorse. Most important, when diversity is deployed in a symbolic manner, the university can purport to demonstrate how hard it is working to be transformative, but in actuality, it is blocked and remains unchanged.

The work to appear not-racist is too often the motivating factor for 'doing diversity.' When those who are brought into the institution create an appearance of diversity, they are assumed to do so with a smile, grateful face, or what Ahmed (2012, 2017) articulates as 'embodying the commitment to diversity.' Black, Indigenous staff and students of Colour are often asked to smile for brochures and posters. However, this smile that claims to represent diversity is a form of recession, a withdrawal, a concession for their inclusion. The smile symbolises a fantasy. Ahmed argues that 'doing diversity' is then seen as a form of repair, a way to acknowledge that although racism may have been a part of its history, it is not a current part of the institutional life of the university. By solely focusing on representation (adding diversity, with its nebulous meaning) without attending to the structural, historical, and institutional factors that precede the need and desire to 'diversify,' universities are engaging with it performatively, rather than in meaningful ways that may work towards transforming the inherent whiteness of the institution. Within this context, doing diversity can be conceptualised as a regime.

Thomas (2018) describes a *diversity regime*:

> A diversity regime is a set of meanings and practices that institionalises benign commitments to diversity, and in doing so, obscures, entrenches, and even intensifies existing racial inequality by failing to make fundamental changes in how power, resources, and opportunities are distributed (p.141).

If 'doing diversity' is part of a regime, it is not surprising to see the failure of any altering of the philosophies or policies within the existing infrastructures of the university. The regime runs on hegemonic notions of what and how the university should exist and function, i.e., upholding and maintaining systems of whiteness in its many manifestations and forms. Thus, within the context of the white university, aiming for diversity must be questioned in its authenticity as it is often idealistic, misunderstood, and reactionary. Desiring diversity exposes how society both wants it (whatever 'it' means) yet is also threatened by 'it' as soon as there is any indication that power and hierarchy have the potential to be upended and challenged.

As institutions of higher education discuss their engagement with diversity, their desire is not so much racial diversity as it is to not be seen as racist against contemporary discourse that engages with social justice and diversity. The fear of being called or deemed racist is often of more concern than working to dismantle systems and structures that speak to *how* and *why* the university upholds racist structures and attitudes. When institutions 'desire diversity,' they believe they are responding to calls for the need to diversify but only do so as much as it does not threaten or disrupt the status quo of the whiteness within the university. Additionally, when rhetoric that claims the want and need to diversify intersects with little or no context as to why the university is taking up this call, things can backfire, resulting in dangerous and unsafe work environments for those who have been brought in to 'diversify.'

As Patel (2015) argues, when people believe they receive privileges based on hard work and/or inherent superiority, they feel resentment when perceiving that their entitlement is threatened by those they deem as less worthy, i.e., people brought in as a 'diversity hire.' When the morality of diversity coincides with institutional values such as meritocracy, the result can create a volatile environment that is unsafe and even more discriminatory. Non-white inferiority relies on the social construction of race to uphold stereotypes for sorting and relying on assumptions and social ascriptions. Simultaneously, universities that claim they are race-neutral spaces whilst working to diversify actually reinforce their whiteness and power, thus resulting in maintaining whiteness. Not surprisingly, diversity is not the only term or concept deployed to uphold whiteness on university campuses.

What happens when universities choose to engage the term colour-blindness (as opposed to diversity) when responding to critiques about the whiteness of their respective institutions? The term colour-blindness is as nebulous as diversity, as it discounts and undermines the social construction of race and its' real-life ramifications whilst doubling down on individuality and the omnipresent nature of whiteness and racial domination. Colour-blindness is engaged as another strategy to counter the criticism directed at universities for enabling racist and discriminatory practices and policies. What follows is a multi-faceted discussion and analysis of the term colour-blindness, which I argue reinforces, masks, and normalises the whiteness of the university.

Colour-blindness[3]

Like diversity, the term colour-blindness is nuanced, geographic, and context-specific. It traverses the political spectrum depending on its usage and purpose. Recognising the normative operation of race and racism in geographical, physical, and cultured spaces, colour-blindness serves to uphold whiteness and is integral to racialised social systems of global anti-Black racism that ensure whites' fantasies of complete domination over place and space (Embrick & Moore, 2020, also see Norris, as interviewed in Yancy, 2023, and Andres, 2018.). Maintaining white space is fundamental to the reproduction and sustainability of white supremacy, particularly within the context of the university, as education is just a microcosm of society. These white spaces become impenetrable due to the confusing rhetoric of the university that purports to be aiming towards challenging racism whilst reinforcing white superiority. All the while, hegemonically white spaces characterise non-white inferiority as normative and expected. In other words, colour-blind language deployed by universities is so cleverly crafted, that even those within these spaces who believe they are working for an institution that appears to care about dismantling oppressive and racist structures, often fail to see any substantive change or transformation. Just as the members of the forest community know their assigned roles, so do the members of education communities. Complacency is too easy when you have been fed a convincing narrative that things can and will change, but nothing changes and everyone and everything is existing and behaving just as they should be.

It is not enough to simply state that colour-blindness upholds whiteness and racial domination. Colour-blindness is often misunderstood, as it has been used in many different contexts over the last few decades. Although some of its initial meanings do not resonate as they used to (I don't see colour), the current manner in which a colour-blind ideology is deployed still works as an effective strategy to keep the whiteness of the university intact and thriving.

Recently, the term colour- blindness has 'rebranded' itself by arguing that its purpose is to provide everyone with an equal opportunity to succeed and be judged on 'who they are' and 'what they do,' rather than receiving preferential treatment based on racial ascription or identification. However, by denying the

---

[3] Parts of this section are drawn from de Saxe (2022).

existence and reality of race and colourism (Walker, 1983), there is a refusal to see how racial categorisation marginalises and dehumanises, both with in and out-group discrimination.

Colourism, theorised by Walker, reinforces a differential treatment and prejudice based on phenotype and proximity to whiteness. Relatedly, Mills (1997) iterates that race becomes a system that places people in different spots with respect to the system. This system is context and location-specific, which is connected to phenotype, resulting in how one is treated within a specific location, time, geography, and politic. These systems vary, as one might assume a different race depending on the country, politics, and culture of a place. This context and socially constructed system does not denote race as insignificant or neutral. In fact, race is very real. Where one is slotted within a particular racialised system dictates whom they can marry, their life chances, education, etc. Race as a social construct matters hugely, thus, to suggest that individuality is the only way to judge one in an objective way completely disregards the interconnectivity between the social construction of race and its real-life consequences and ramifications.

In as much, the power of colour-blindness within the university system is that it obscures the fact that institutional and structural racism are entrenched within all aspects of university education; admission requirements, diversity statements, course offerings, as well as who holds full-time positions as lecturers and professors (Bonilla-Silva, 2015, Burke, 2017; Lipsitz, 2019; McAllister, 2019; Rollock, 2018; Naepi, 2019). Within a colour-blind framework, race shouldn't matter, as it seemingly reinforces an individual approach to race relations (Bonilla-Silva, 2003; Warikoo & Novais, 2015). However, to reiterate, with this one -dimensional and simplistic understanding, the real-life consequences of access, power, and privilege are seen as mutually exclusive rather than inclusive and intimately interconnected.

The power and subversive nature of a colour-blind ideology is that it reinforces the idea that *opportunity* is colour-blind and that one can claim not to see race, whilst explaining racial inequality without even mentioning racism. Colour-blindness downplays overt and covert racist practices by assuming that it is specifically focused on a racialised other. Within this underdeveloped interpretation, there is an abdication of responsibility from whites in seeing their own racial ascription, as within a colour-blind ideology, race then becomes meaningless for everyone. Whites both consciously and subconsciously fail to locate themselves on the racial hierarchy, as by doing so, they would have to 'see colour.'

Colour-blindness is racist in that it normalises whiteness. However, it is not racist in and of itself. As Doane (2017) argues, colour-blind racism exists because it serves to obfuscate reality, whilst supporting and upholding systems of white supremacy. Eddo-Lodge (2017) further argues that the claim to not see race may seem progressive, but it is just another way to reinforce compulsory assimilation. In essence, colour- blindness itself functions as a form of racism, as its ideology minimises (and ignores) both covert and overt acts of racism that allow it to persist (Beaman and Petts, 2020; Bonilla-Silva, 2003 2015; Jayakumar & Adamian, 2017, Lipsitz, 2019). Circumventing conversations about race exerts more energy than addressing race and racism head-on. It takes so much more effort to avoid discussing race when excusing away academic tracking, school success rates, and the stark and obvious contrast in opportunities for students based solely on happenstance and individual work ethic rather than race or racism.

Furthermore, colour-blindness, as an ideology, works to minimise whiteness and highlight an 'other' (Black, Indigenous and People of Colour). As Haymes (1996) argues, to understand racial identity formation, one needs to appreciate the way white is discursively represented as the opposite of Black-a reflection of the Western tendency to privilege one concept in binary opposition to another. Whites gain knowledge of themselves as the racial barometer by which other groups are measured against. Race as a pivotal aspect of one's life seems to exist only within a racially diverse group or experience. It is why so many whites feel free to claim that they do not have culture or race or have never had to talk about culture or race, as their upbringing was 'only with other whites.' A homogenous grouping of whites is seen as raceless until a Black, Indigenous, or Person of Colour is present. When white is considered the norm, it goes unmarked and goes unnoticed.

Additionally, Doane (2017) notes that colour-blindness provides an ideological tool kit that can be used to defend white supremacy by denying the existence of racism and presenting 'nonracist' counterarguments to policy proposals. This line of thinking falls within the belief that discussing race *promotes* racism. I remember in one of my sociology classes a white student shared that she felt like she couldn't talk about race or racism, as she was afraid that she would be considered racist by discussing it. She noted that race was always deemed a taboo topic in her family, social and educational circles, as she was made to believe that naming something would make it 'too real'. I understood her comment to suggest that by discussing and naming race and racism, she would be calling out whiteness, thus making other whites around her uncomfortable and defensive. Previously discussed through the practice of 'white talk,' it is a privilege and a choice for whites to address race and whiteness. Conversely, by avoiding discussing race, power is maintained, and race-neutral language can go back to redressing racial inequalities and promote racial justice through fairness and equality; colour-blind terms that obfuscate the reality of power as it relates to race and whiteness. Through this superficial understanding of colour blindness, the consequences are not only more insidious but also more dangerous.

Said another way, Beaman and Petts (2020) argue that by providing colour-blind explanations for clear racial inequalities, individuals can maintain a level of ignorance about how race is produced and constructed. Ultimately, this reinforces unnamed structures of power, privilege, and access. The perpetuation of racial ideologies and practices depends on an agreed-upon refusal to know so that racial privilege is maintained. In fact, colour-blindness continues to manifest as a dominant and hegemonic racial ideology, as both individuals and society can claim that race is inconsequential in their interactions with others as well as for broader outcomes within society. If race is not explicitly discussed, it must not be present. However, racial ideologies are only racist in as much as they maintain racialised social systems, keeping the hierarchy intact and thriving.

To situate colour-blindness and its impact on the university in our current moment, I discuss and interconnect three ideas: *an epistemology of white ignorance, hegemonic whiteness, and neoliberal racism.* All three demonstrate the subversive nature of colour-blindness, reinforcing the myth of meritocracy, opportunity, and 'equality for all.' These ideas further demonstrate the power and normalisation of the white university, as collectively they double down on individual achievement and merit, whilst assuming that the playing field is levelled. I engage each term philosophically, as well as how they manifest in practice, as both must be understood to deliberately interrupt and challenge a colour-blind ideology both within and outside the white university.

Epistemology of White Ignorance

An epistemology of ignorance, or white ignorance, functions to mystify the consequences of unjust systems that systematically marginalised groups endure so that those who benefit from the system do not need to consider their complicity in perpetuating them (Applebaum, 2019; Mills, 1997, 2007). White ignorance is maintained by social structures and institutions that sustain epistemic injustice on both a structural and individual level. White ignorance not only puts the onus on the marginalised to explain their oppression, but it also manifests by refusing to believe the marginalised (Applebaum, 2019; Berenstain, 2016; Norris, 2019). Within this context, ignorance is not defined as having a lack of knowledge or intellect. Instead, the term ignorance is deployed to maintain racial privilege in ways that are hidden so it doesn't expose what it is actually doing. Although often perpetuated unintentionally, upon close inspection, it becomes clear that by ignoring the power of 'knowing,' members of the dominant group have a vested interest in 'not knowing' (de Saxe, 2021).

This point is best articulated by Applebaum (2019), who states, "the refusal to know allows the systematically privileged to misunderstand and misinterpret the world" (p. 34). This misinterpretation and maintenance of ignorance upholds the status quo by stratifying, privileging, and denoting whiteness as invisible (Morrison, 1992; Leonardo, 2015). Mills (1997) further notes that an epistemology of white ignorance relies on marginalised and oppressed communities to internalise and come to accept their subordinate position and status within the hierarchy of whiteness and privilege. This falls in line with the belief that success is equated with whiteness and that the only way to aspire towards this path of success is to accept one's inferior status. An epistemology of ignorance requires acquiescence, as well as an agreed-upon interpretation of the status quo of whiteness and one's place within the racial hierarchy.

Through this interpretation, an epistemology of ignorance upholds the adage, 'the more you know, the more you don't know.' Jones (2001) connects this idea with having a 'passion for ignorance.' She argues, "the disjunction between two words 'passion' and 'ignorance' make this phrase powerful, especially in relation to university education, which is assumed to be passionately *against* 'ignorance' (p.141). A 'passion for ignorance,' within an Aotearoa New Zealand context can be seen from the reactions by New Zealand European university students who resist the idea that there could be limits to their (western) knowledge. Through this 'passion for ignorance,' as well as within the context of general histories of racism, the term connotes a subtle form of racism and discourse, particularly in nations that define themselves as socially liberal and multicultural.

An epistemology of white ignorance is also protected through an upholding of colour-blindness. Burke (2017) articulates this point well:

When we study individuals, we must consider *how* they make meaning of the worlds that surround them, and also the ways that activity based on that meaning may work in the service of larger oppressive or liberatory practices, where material consequences are produced (p. 859).

Succumbing to colour-blind thinking also supports white student' positive self-image, upholding their personal sense of success and status and protecting them from feeling underserving of their privileges. Burke (2017) notes that even within progressive circles, many are grappling with the ideas of colour-blindness- that race should not matter- alongside the reality that it actually does. Within this worldview, whites have the capacity to live anonymously, to go unmarked and unnamed. Whiteness, then, becomes normalised and hegemonic.

An epistemology of white ignorance does not produce cognitive dissonance for those with power and privilege because it is rooted in a hegemonic understanding of a world steeped in normalising whiteness (de Saxe, 2021; Storch, E. A. & Storch, J. B, 2003). This is why individual reforms cannot in and of themselves lead to epistemic justice unless they coincide and interconnect with structural and institutional transformation. Orozco (2016) argues that individual whites may claim innocence (and ignorance) from engaging in personal participation in equity initiatives such as housing, school integration, etc., doubling down on their misinterpretation of their innocence and the very real de facto segregation that persists within such initiatives. Consequently, the very systems that many whites purport to work on changing and transforming are upheld by and maintained by their wilful innocence. Applebaum (2015) highlights this paradox of white innocence and proclamations of benevolence. She states,

> In what might seem like a paradox, white benevolence is an important site to interrogate the type of problem that white complicity is. White benevolence not only comes with implicit requisite demands but might also function to silence those upon whom benevolence is bestowed. Because benevolence is considered 'good,' the one who bestows the benevolence has in effect secured his/her innocence and does not have to questions his/her implication of injustice (p.3).

An epistemology of white ignorance and the teaching and learning of white supremacy can be a slippery slope into recentring whiteness if white educators and their students fail to implicate themselves in what they critique. Through the intentional ambiguity of a white supremacist matrix (Yancy, 2012), whites can insidiously explain away their complicity in upholding whiteness. Applebaum (2022) builds on the ambiguity of white supremacy, which she argues is fundamental to upholding the many dimensions of whiteness. In fact, this ambiguity is what allows many whites to abdicate responsibility in claiming their racism, as too often, white racial enlightenment comes with the othering of whites less 'advanced' in their white racial awareness. As Yancy so firmly declares, anti-racist whites can still be white racists. Within the context of the 'good white,' one's awareness towards their white racial consciousness can easily derail into a performative act when failing to connect good intentions with being complicit in the larger system of white racial domination.

Finally, Jayakumar and Adamian (2016) note that even within white students' ability to understand and align with racially progressive and theoretically nuanced understandings of structural racism and whiteness, as well as counternarratives that challenge racial hierarchy, they still disconnect from a critical analysis of their own racial standpoint and positionality, experiences and/or actions. White students too often have the privilege to flee the discomfort of 'difficult knowledge' that challenges their moral integrity, as then they would be asked to consider their role in the reproduction of white supremacy. Thus, it is vital to unpack structural, hegemonic, and institutional whiteness within the university context so that students can aim for a wider and more nuanced lens in which to consider their own complicity.

Hegemonic Whiteness

When people claim they don't see race, it often means they do not see those who are assumed to bring race with them (white: not of colour; race: of colour). "I don't see race" thus translates as: I don't see not white. (Ahmed, 2017, p. 119).

White supremacy functions because hegemonic whiteness relies on the collective social force (as opposed to individual whites) that shapes the lives of whites as well as the lives of racial minorities. Within a hegemonic interpretation of whiteness, there is a common-sense and an agreed upon narrative that normalises whiteness; it becomes unchecked due to its unmarkable force. Yancy (2012) speaks to this by asking to whom is whiteness invisible? He returns white people to the problem of whiteness by shouting "Look a White!" This proclamation is an intentional flipping of the script of Fanon's experience of a young white boy 'seeing' him and shouting, "Look, a Negro!" (Fanon, 1967). Fanon feels the impact of the collective white gaze. In this situation, he becomes a dreaded object, a thing of fear, a frightening and ominous presence. This pointing is the power of racial gesturing and an expression that calls forth an entire white racist worldview. By ignoring racist practices and structures through the hegemony of whiteness, the status of whites as racial actors is undermined whilst simultaneously suggesting that 'having race' is only for racialised others (BIPOC).

The world of whiteness is implicit as a default version of living comfortably in society (Matias & Mackey, 2016; Mills, 1997, 2015; Yancy, 2012). As Lewis (2004) argues, whiteness includes an interworking of practices and meanings that occupy and reinforce the dominant position in a particular racial formation. The insidious nature of hegemonic whiteness is that it successfully occupies the empty (yet loaded) space of 'normalcy' in everyday structures. Whiteness is seen as a clear but opaque social construction that elevates the status of people on the racial hierarchy considered white at any given point in history. Within this default status and version of what is 'normal,' whiteness is the lens through which other bodies are viewed as 'of colour' and, thus, racialised. Lewis further iterates, "whites social location (i.e., their status as racial actors as part of the racial hierarchy) is always present whether or not it is ever actively taken up or becomes self-consciously salient (p. 628)". The power of hegemonic whiteness is that it normalises the process of whites viewing and othering BIPOC, as opposed to asking whites to see how they understand their own racial selves and their unearned status.

Additionally, by understanding how an ideology and normalisation of whiteness trickles down to the many aspects of the university culture, such as course options, syllabi, hiring decisions and student demographics (just to name a few), its power and omnipresent nature become quite clear. These understandings often lead students to experience cognitive dissonance, often challenging the 'good white/not racist' persona they believe to be. It is too easy for students not to listen. Through critical learning and interrogating the hegemony of whiteness, therein lies the potential to move whites into a space of white racial consciousness that asks them to make sense of their own racial selves and their earned/unearned status.

Bonilla-Silva (2003) further argues that whiteness is the visible uniform of the dominant racial group. Whites (as a dominant group) can live and 'do race' without even actually being self-conscious or aware of it. When white people say they don't have race, what they are demonstrating is a hegemonic and agreed-upon notion of understanding whiteness, ultimately reinforcing its opaqueness and existence solely in juxtaposition to blackness (de Saxe, 2021). As just one example, the slogan All Lives Matter in contrast to Black Lives Matter doubles down on the inability to see well- documented and stark disparities in the criminal justice system and over- policing of Black lives. By simply suggesting that Black Lives Matter, the fear and vitriol espoused by whites demonstrate the threat they feel when illuminating the exposure of colour-blindness. Lewis (2004) explains this well by noting that "the 'blackness' of blacks is more often an object of focus than the 'whiteness' of whites".

Subversively, hegemonic whiteness does not ask how whites understand their whiteness and privileges that may lead directly to their unearned status and 'successes,' particularly within the context of education. It is a choice for whites to interrogate their own privilege and its relationship to how they view their own successes. This protection and evasiveness are what upholds and maintains the walls of whiteness and its hegemony. As a result, the university sustains a colour-blind ideology through neoliberal racism by conceptualising education through individual achievement and merit, racism, as well as a white lens and framework (Darder, 2012; Guissa, 2010; Kidman, 2019). What follows is a discussion of neoliberal racism and its role in perpetuating a colour-blind ideology within academia.

Neoliberal Racism

Education from a neoliberal approach puts a premium on individuality, competition and self-meritocracy as captured by the 'pull oneself up by the bootstraps' metaphor. If one tries as hard as they can, they should be able to succeed. If not, it must be the fault of the individual for not working hard enough. These goals reinforce the seemingly neutral characteristics of individualism and standardisation within education, framing them as inherently part of the process, as opposed to something that must be questioned and challenged (de Saxe, 2016). Neoliberalism pays little attention to societal inequities and multiple forms of marginalisation and oppression, as meritocracy is seen and framed as fair and democratic. Better stated by Gordon (2022), under the [neoliberal] rubric, privatisation valorises abstract and moralistic notions of the "individual as though each person is an individual god capable of determining the conditions of their needs by themselves" (p.11). This perspective is quite subversive, as by doubling down on individual accountability, it becomes easy to justify who is 'worthy' of existing within academic spaces.

Neoliberal racism is just one way that a colour-blind ideology thrives within the university, as within this context, the social structures and policies that are directly related to colour-blindness are ignored in lieu of individual acts of racism and exclusion. A racist neoliberal ideology seeks to colonise, suppress, and reinforce the fear that any form of critical thinking within the university might uncover racism, as well as challenge the status quo of complacency, individualism, and inequity (Bargh, 2007; Darder, 2012; de Saxe, 2021). A neoliberal ideology places blame directly on the individual when it comes to defining 'success' and 'failure.' Picower and Mayorga (2015) note that there is a connective tissue that is continually being forged between ideologies, intentions, and the formation of policies and practices. This must be understood as an amalgamation of insidious practices and ways of thinking about the world that directly interconnect and dehumanise elements of race, class, gender, and sexuality, among other identifiers.

Neoliberalism upholds the university as a colonising structure by pushing back on 'diversity politics' and radical voices from the margins: cultural, racialised, economic, gendered, and sexual borderlands. Even when the university structures purport to 'decolonise,' in reality, they work to reinforce their problematic histories into the contemporary everyday. As Kidman (2019) argues, "in New Zealand, where there are widespread and uncomfortable silences about the colonial past, settler-colonial and neoliberal forces cooperate within a grid of power relations that connect historical and modern forms of coloniality with market-driven ideologies (p. 52)". Additionally, neoliberalism demonstrates a translation of many older colonial beliefs, once expressed explicitly, now expressed implicitly, into language, practices, and philosophies that are actually far more covert about their civilising mission (Bargh, 2007). The hegemonic and colonising structures of the university prioritise self-meritocracy by denying the workings of racism and privilege in favour of discourses of merit and blame.

Within a neoliberal ideology, the university fails to provide students an opportunity where they can learn to think critically, engage with others, and work to challenge institutional whiteness and colour-blindness. In fact, too many students leave university unprepared to make transformative contributions and resist policies and practices that reinforce stark inequities in society because they have been trained to stay within the confines of what counts as 'knowledge' (Apple and Buras, 2006; Giroux, 2001; 2012). Even more troubling, the university often presents itself as being beyond the perpetuation of racial inequality, ignoring the connection between hostile campus environments and the maintenance of colour-blindness. When those in power deny the existence of their own prejudice and invalidate the experiences of the marginalised, they are, in fact, demonstrating a colour-blind racial ideology. The tenets that uphold a colour-blind ideology (epistemology of white ignorance, hegemonic whiteness, and neoliberal racism) perpetuate a philosophy of evasion and denial of their impact on individuals and the university writ large.

Conclusion

Challenging university structures, policies, and practices (particularly within volatile and openly hostile environments) requires more than just naming and promising to change and work to transform. Particularly within the context of diversity and colour-blind rhetoric, universities must do and be better at deliberately and proactively interrogating the inherent whiteness that works to obfuscate the realities of both overt and covert forms of racism and discrimination. However, all too often, those who experience and call out racism are seen as the problem. In fact, in an incredible twist of irony, by making those who experience racism the problem (*they must be paranoid!*), racism does not become the problem (Ahmed, 2017, italics added). The following quote articulates this point well:

> It is because of how racism saturates everyday and institutional spaces that POC often make strategic decisions not to use the language of racism. If you already pose as a problem or appear 'out of place' in the institutions of whiteness, there can be good reasons not to exercise what is heard as a threatening or aggressive vocabulary (Ahmed, 2017, p 162).

It is naive to suggest that by simply naming racism and racist behaviour, the university (as an institution) will actively work towards dismantling and challenging it. The university is not a safe space to share experiences of racism and discrimination. Not only is it a place where minoritised students and professors experience hostile behaviour, but when they do directly confront such experiences, they are not believed, and the narrative is flipped to place the blame on those who are on the receiving end of the behaviour. However, within the context and ethos of the third-prong, as well as the philosophy of this book, I argue that we can deploy critical theory, tools, and modes of educational resistance to disrupt and challenge whiteness and racial domination within the university. This third prong speaks to the power of a multi-dimensional and multi-faceted approach to interrogating whiteness from an individual, communal and institutional perspective. It demonstrates the liberating potential of education, resistance and transformation.

Chapter 5

Critical Race Theory and *Testimonio* (Three-pronged approach question 3- How do we respond to, work to transform, and/or undermine the 'problem'?)

Introduction

The previous chapter discussed the concepts of diversity and colour blindness, both of which uphold and reinforce whiteness within the university. Too often, when these terms are deployed to confront and name whiteness and racism from within, they actually result in the opposite, reinforcing behaviours that subjugate and marginalise faculty and students. This discriminatory and racist behaviour often manifests in openly hostile and harmful ways. However, not all oppression is overt. The more subtle and 'casual' means by which Black, Indigenous, and People of Colour are marginalised are just as dehumanising.

Significantly, it is incomplete to talk about oppression without discussing resistance and fighting back. Thus, I draw on and engage critical race theory and *testimonio,* as both speak to undermining and talking back to the overt and subversive behaviours that BIPOC students and staff experience within the white university. The first section of this chapter speaks to this type of behaviour, also called epistemic exploitation, which demonstrates some of the subversive ways that diversity and colour blindness (drawing from the previous chapter) reinforce whiteness and racial domination within the university context. Specifically, I pay close attention to how epistemic exploitation and racial microaggressions are harmful experiences for those on the receiving end, as well as how such behaviours reinforce an 'o'ther, a 'body out of place,' and a 'problem' within the university.

As Delgado Bernal (2002) argues, the nature of the university is that the educational structures, processes, and discourses operate in contradictory ways as they not only oppress and marginalise but they also demonstrate the potential to emancipate and empower. As such, I respond to epistemic exploitation and racial microaggressions by contradicting such behaviours with tools that are emancipatory and empowering. I examine critical race theory and *testimonio*, both of which directly and actively undermine educational spaces that are anything but liberatory and transformative. Thus, the purpose of chapter five is to situate and discuss specific behaviours that dehumanise and marginalise, then follow with some ways to counter and disrupt these behaviours through modes of resistance that aim to transform the university from a place of oppression to one of liberation.

Epistemic Exploitation

Despite Maehe's personal experiences and research about racism, the White male felt he had the authority to tell her that she needed to follow directions from another White male. Interesting...Later, she reflects more deeply about what the finger-pointing was really about. Underneath the range of fragile responses and excuses was a clear message: you are the problem, not us. Not the racism of the university (MacDonald as cited in Stewart et.al, 2023).

Within the context of university education, there is a reliance on upholding overt forms of racism and discrimination, as well as the more subtle degradations and putdowns in order to maintain the status quo of dominant ideologies and epistemologies of whiteness. Examining epistemology cannot occur without considering the dimensions of power (Applebaum, 2018). Thus, I begin this section with a discussion and analysis of epistemic exploitation. To reiterate, epistemology (or something that is epistemic) is how one comes to know what they know. Why does one know what they know, and why do they believe it is true? Exploitation, or exploiting someone, is the act or action of treating someone in a harmful and unfair manner and then benefiting from their work. The term epistemic exploitation refers to taking someone's knowledge (intentionally and/or unintentionally) and gaining this knowledge through the emotional and cognitive labour of the person whose knowledge has been taken. When epistemically exploitative practices are conceived as only about offence, the role that systematically privileged subjects play in maintaining systemic ignorance can remain hidden (Applebaum, 2018; Kidman & Chu, 2019; Smith et al., 2022).

Epistemic exploitation towards Black Indigenous and People of Colour undermines epistemic agency and experiences, and through subversive power-plays and virtuosity, active ignorance, whiteness, and racial domination are maintained and reproduced (Applebaum, 2019; Mills 1997, 2015; Yancy, 2012). Epistemic exploitation occurs when questioning one's credibility and ability to remember and accurately portray an experience of oppression. Within this situation, knowledge is discredited and undermined, as the marginalised are often accused of misremembering an incident and their experience, not believed, and are told they are over-reacting. One's epistemic agency is not respected or, more accurately stated, is fully disrespected.

To add a double burden, the person on the receiving end of epistemically exploitative behaviour is seen and tasked with being the spokesperson for the entire community to which they belong. Thus, not only is one's personal experience of racism discounted and discredited, but they become the representative for an entire group and, by default, are also viewed as suspect. This further intensifies the gymnastics-like behaviour of epistemic exploitation; the oppressed are seen as making something up whilst simultaneously tokenised and speaking for an entire community. As a result, all members of their group must make up their experiences with racism and discrimination. As Applebaum (2018) argues, the systematically privileged can continue to remain ignorant as the marginalised experiences remain unintelligible to them. Further, the reliving of an experience causes stress and results in situations in which the marginalised must decide how to counter and respond to the circumstances in which they find themselves. One's emotional labour is being exploited and discredited simultaneously (Applebaum, 2019; Berenstain, 2016; Dotson, 2011&2014). In fact, the insidious nature of whiteness and its relationship to diversity and colour-blindness is that calling out discrimination often turns the problem onto the person experiencing the racist behaviour as opposed to the perpetrator (Ahmed, 2012; 2017).

For example, when someone experiences racism within the university and is subsequently asked to recall the incident, they are often not believed, told they are making a big deal out of nothing, or are too sensitive. With the risk of perpetuating stereotypes and stereotype threat, those who experience racism and share their experience with others often worry about being cast as being 'too defensive,' or reacting in a way that further downplays the racist incident. The response by the dominant group is that the experience must be a one-off or a misinterpretation. This raises doubt about a person's ability to accurately perceive and understand events. Being characterised as 'overly sensitive' can also result in losing one's epistemic grounding, resulting in the questioning of one's own experience and interpretation of their experience (Berenstain, 2016; Norris, 2019).

This interaction, more the norm than the exception, demonstrates an undermining of the epistemic agency of the subjugated. The responses from the person who asks for the testimony place blame on the victim, arguing that their behaviour is what should be questioned, and thus, their experience is too often delegitimised and questioned. The twist of irony in this situation is that the testimony from the victim is often solicited as the needed evidence to challenge racism within the university, but through epistemic exploitation, the act of testifying serves to reinforce the narrative that marginalised academics, staff, and students who call out racist and discriminatory behaviours are in fact seen as the 'problem' and become the object of blame, rather than taking the testimony as the necessary evidence of racism.

Further, epistemic exploitation keeps the oppressed busy doing the oppressors' work by treating existing oppressive systems (i.e., the university) as up for debate as opposed to being institutionalised and reproduced. As a form of gaslighting, the marginalised are tasked with the emotionally exhausting work of reliving demeaning and dehumanising experiences whilst having to defend these experiences, often taking a toll on their mental and physical health and well-being. These epistemically exploitative interactions often occur in university classrooms with just one or a few Black, Indigenous, or Students of Colour, and where they are tokenised and asked to speak for and on behalf of the marginalised group to which they belong. This personal experience is then used as a universal perspective, which, not surprisingly, is not done nor asked of by white students.

Even more insidious, upon hearing a story or personal experience from a marginalised person, members of the dominant group may centre their own whiteness and fragility by expressing guilt, defensiveness, and tears, ultimately taking the focus away from the oppressed and the knowledge they share. The marginalised then must succumb to prioritising white feelings and dealing with the mental acrobatics of comforting the person who is epistemically exploiting them. In response to this form of emotional exhaustion, Reni Eddo-Lodge wrote the following post in her blog in 2017:

> I'm no longer talking to white people about race... The balance is too far swung in their favour. Their intent is often not to listen or learn, but to exert their power, to prove me wrong, to emotionally drain me, and to rebalance the status quo.

Epistemic exploitation, or epistemically exploitative behaviour, can also be described as casual racism or racial microaggressions. These are often not taken seriously, as they can be perceived as more subtle and framed as less harmful. Conversely, they are quite an insidious and dangerous form of racism. Both individual and institutional racial microaggressions are intimately interconnected to and rely upon the subversive ways that epistemic exploitation manifests.

Racial Microaggressions

Even in seemingly progressive and 'critical' university spaces, it is too easy for racial microaggressions to be downplayed and even explained away as racism that is 'out there' as opposed to 'in here.' Racial microaggressions are innocuous, preconscious, or unconscious degradations, and putdowns, often kinetic, but capable of being verbal and/or kinetic. In and of itself, a racial microaggression may seem harmless, but the cumulative burden of a lifetime of them can theoretically contribute to diminished mortality, augmented morbidity, and flattened confidence (Yosso et.al. 2010). Microaggressions are discursive practices that serve to undermine the thoughts and feelings of Black, Indigenous, and People of Colour, in which the perpetrator is seemingly oblivious of their effects. Sue et al. (2008) further argue that the subtle nature of individual microaggressions can result in a dismissal of the microaggression, often framing it as non-existent, a miscommunication, or even an overreaction, i.e., epistemically exploitative behaviour. Additionally, trivialising the effects of microaggressions functions as a guise for not hearing. Applebaum (2019) argues that not taking microaggressions seriously is just another form of upholding systemic and white ignorance that continues to silence the perspective and experiences of the marginalised. The consequence of this silencing is that it is often difficult to locate and make evident, as it is hard to show and 'demonstrate' evidence to prove such silencing, particularly as it relates to self-silencing (Dotson, 2011; 2014). Eddo-Lodge (2017) adds that self-silencing scares oneself from speaking honestly about their feelings without assessing the consequences.

Racial microaggressions further reinforce the status quo of whiteness that is often excused away, ignored, or downplayed. They do not occur in abstraction from white supremacist racial structures and are inextricably linked to those structures (Johnson & Joseph-Salisbury, 2018). The white university perpetuates racial microaggressions at the macro level through course offerings, privileging western and dominant epistemologies and one-dimensional forms of assessment, just to name a few. These structures and systems within the university are designed to reproduce and maintain the ethos of the white privileged elite. Otherwise known as an element of the 'hidden curriculum,'[1] institutional microaggressions are often harder to see and call out due to their normalising and hegemonic nature within the university culture. Like the hegemony of the academy, traditional westernised schooling and institutional microaggressions are powerful forces that too many students and academics experience for often many years of their time in school. Better stated, Andrews (2018) argues that the university is not racist- the university *is* racism.

Casual racism within the university is also fluid and commonplace (Arday, 2017). Racial microaggressions are always in iteration with institutional and macro white supremacy and are often normalised by the same systems that claim to challenge them. (Applebaum, 2019; Orozco & Jaime Diaz, 2016). As Smith et al. (2022) argue, the university's coloniality machinery continues to thrive by perpetrating colonial microaggressions when asked to alter pedagogy or philosophies that even slightly challenge whiteness and settler colonialism. By upholding white and active ignorance, there is a sophisticated effort to not only suppress accurate information but also to distribute false information (Berenstain, 2016). Additionally, dehumanising and oppressive campus racial climates create anxiety to the point that many students can't shake the sense that their every word potentially reaffirms racialised assumptions that cast doubt on their academic merit. Arday adds, "racial microaggressions are often utilised as a tool of whiteness to demonstrate that Blacks are not as capable as their white counterparts" (p.173). In other words, whiteness and the subtle occurrences of subordination are intimately interconnected and result in a burden that accompanies BIPOC students and staff throughout their experiences at university. This epistemically exploitative behaviour resembles the invisibility and hyper-surveillance of 'bodies out of place' and an 'outsider within.'

To further the intersection between epistemic exploitation, racial microaggressions, and a 'body out of place,' I draw on the work of Johnson & Joseph-Salisbury (2020), who argue that a 'body out of place' is both invisible and

---

[1] I refer to Rick and William Ayers and their discussion of a hidden curriculum in their book, *Teaching the Taboo: Courage and Imagination in the classroom*. They argue, "the hidden curriculum-all the unstated assumptions, beliefs, and values that prop up the culture and the structure of every school- works its own mighty will. Because it's opaque, unavailable for comment or critique, it is often a more powerful teacher than the official and planned curriculum" (p.29).

hypervisible, creating a space for racial microaggressions to occur. The 'not belonging' within the white university is inherently part of how white supremacist structures are upheld at the micro and macro levels. Souto – Manning and Ray (2007) further argue "both individualised and institutionalised oppressive forces operate in tandem with one another and can have a tremendous impact on the academic success and well-being of graduate Women of Colour" (p.282). How does a Black, Indigenous, Student or Professor of Colour feel a sense of belonging not only in a sea of whiteness, but having to speak of their personal experience for an entire group of people only to have this experience explained away and undermined through whiteness? Through a Duboisan lens, BIPOC academics and students are aware of how they are perceived within a university that relies on epistemic exploitation and institutional microaggressions that uphold structural and hegemonic whiteness within the university space. Ahmed further engages this point by arguing, "if you already pose as a problem, or appear 'out of place' in the institutions of whiteness, there can be good reason not to exercise what is heard as threatening or aggressive vocabulary" (p. 162, 2017). Every behaviour, reaction, and engagement within the university is seen as suspect and in direct opposition to a community that is socially, politically, and historically constructed and upheld through a white lens and framework.

How can subjugate knowledges ever be legitimised when the bodies that hold this knowledge are seen as out of place? By understanding how a 'body out of place' is positioned in stark contrast to the way that white bodies are neutralised, it is clear how epistemic exploitation and racial microaggressions reinforce that Black, Indigenous and People of Colour are seen and framed as trespassers. Additionally, when approaches to scholarship and knowledge fail to see how whiteness dominates 'official knowledge,' epistemic violence is perpetuated and upheld. As subjugated knowledge is often framed as 'less credible,' the assumption from a white, colonial, and western university context is that such knowledge is 'harder to access,' and questioned as being worthy for academia. As Kidman (2019) iterates, Indigenous and Black faculty and their scholarship are perceived as less able, less rational, and less 'civilised' than white academics. This framing subversively provides the academy with a way to rationalise their marginalisation. Even with the highest of academic credentials, a BIPOC academic is still mistaken for anyone but a professor or member of the academic community.

As just one example, someone who is 'curious' and wants to learn more may engage with a Black, Indigenous and/or Academic of Colour, asking them to explain their research, teach them about their ideas, (particularly about race and/or other scholarship on oppression) whilst simultaneously discrediting their work (Kidman, 2019). The virtuosity of this 'learning' not only sits within the good white paradox, (Applebaum, 2021) but it further exposes the power dynamics at play as the marginalised should be 'grateful' that people want to learn about who they are as well as their culture (Berenstain, 2016). All the while, the scholarship they are asking to be taught is readily available and accessible for those who want to learn about it. This is when a situation known as a double bind occurs. A Black, Indigenous and/or Academic of Colour may choose not to engage, knowing that their scholarship and epistemic agency will be questioned and/or potentially challenged and discredited (Arday, 2017; Applebaum, 2018, 2019; Berenstain, 2016; Dotson, 2011, 2014; Eddo-Lodge, 2017; Johnson & Joseph-Salisbury, 2017). However, if they do not partake in this academic and emotionally exhausting labour, they are seen as embodying the stereotypes and pre-subscribed racist tropes that they know are constructed about them. The marginalised are seen as not being willing to teach and explain their research, even though by doing so, their cognitive and academic integrity are both demeaned and exploited. If the oppressors are provided with this knowledge, they are then often praised for their racial awareness and 'new' knowledge acquisition. As Berenstain (2016) articulates,

> The marginalised have sacrificed their time, energy, and expertise in the service of the privileged. The privileged receive social recognition from the newfound knowledge and self-improvement that are rarely conferred on the marginalised persons who produce this knowledge" (p.575).

This newfound knowledge is gifted at the expense of the marginalised. It becomes self-congratulatory for white people, as they now profess their solidarity in 'finally understanding.' But at what cost? Herein lies another catch-22. By keeping the oppressed occupied teaching such knowledge, they have less time to work on their own scholarship and publishing. Individuals from oppressed groups have a choice between cooperating with an oppressive norm, which is bad for them in the long run, or resisting the oppressive norm and suffering some harm or punishment, which undermines their long-term ability to resist oppression (Dunne & Kotsonis, 2023, p.350). The marginalised are also tasked with serving on diversity committees, taking on a higher load of BIPOC students to mentor (among other extra-institutional tasks), all the while knowing that this extra work and labour rarely lead to institutional change.

The importance of calling out and undermining epistemically exploitative behaviours and racial microaggressions cannot be understated. Teaching these two terms in my classes is quite a different experience for each student, depending on their racial standpoints, positionalities, and various identities and personal experiences. Again, this is the power and potential of learning and engaging critical theory; through unpacking terms that help articulate something in a more concrete way, it is easier to name and challenge it. The concept of epistemic exploitation is one that is quite powerful in terms of how students connect with it. Black, Indigenous, and Students of Colour, as well as other marginalised students in class, have shared that by engaging a concept that explains how they feel when asked to share their experiences (and subsequently not believed) is both liberating and healing. For white students, learning about epistemic exploitation and realising how they contribute to this behaviour flips the script for them, in that they come to see the impact of their 'curiosity' and casting doubt. This mind shift, or working towards white racial consciousness, is one of the goals of this book. Moving away from positioning BIPOC faculty and students as ones who must 'teach' and 'instil' knowledge for 'enlightenment,' it is the responsibility of white people to learn and teach themselves. Villenas (2019) argues the privileged must educate themselves and others who are privileged, as they are more likely to believe claims about privilege and oppression when they come from other people who share their privilege. This requires a reframing of the white university to challenge members of the community to take responsibility for educating themselves and others about racism and whiteness.

Undermining the White University

What does it mean to talk back and undermine, and how does this relate to interrupting the many facets of the white university discussed thus far? The next section unpacks critical race theory and *testimonio*, both of which are counternarratives that resist and challenge epistemic exploitation and racial microaggressions. Critical race theory and *testimonio* are counter-stories that confront traditionally white institutions, and dominant paradigms of education, as well as validate experiences that are often relegated to the margins and/or not believed. Significantly, critical race theory and *testimonio* move stories up to the front and serve to deliberately resist, transform, and create a discourse of solidarity; particularly within the context of education.

To re-state, when drawing on any critical theory as a form of liberation, hooks (1994) pays attention to the fact that theory by itself is not inherently healing, liberatory, or revolutionary. It fulfils this function only when one asks that it does so and that it directs such theorising towards this end. To effectively move forward with action and transformation, critical theory must be seen as an extension of practice, as theories do not exist solely for analysing the experiences of others, they coexist within and through anyone who chooses to let them in (Au, 2012; Saavedra and Pérez, 2012). Critical race theory and *testimonio* offer just this. They provide a space to make the abstract more concrete through humanising experiences that expose, share, and bear witness to the consequences of white supremacy on human lives.

Critical Race Theory

As a conceptual tool of resistance, critical race theory has the potential to disrupt and interrogate epistemic exploitation and racial microaggressions. As Villenas (2019) argues, exposing racial microaggressions is a strategy for anti-racist and anti-oppressive work. Critical race theory is part of the active framework that directly undermines an ideology of whiteness by disrupting the educational canon and mainstream academic knowledge and what counts as 'T'ruth, as well as questioning hegemonic understandings of oppression and resistance.

Critical race theory articulated by Derrek Bell in the 1970's, challenges dominant standards of meritocracy, colour-blindness, race neutrality and equality. Bell argues that white supremacy and the subordination of Black, Indigenous, and People of Colour were/are created and maintained through education, law, policies, etc. As an analytical tool of resistance, critical race theory foregrounds race and racism in all aspects of the research and teaching process, as well as challenges the traditional research paradigms, forms of knowledge, texts, and theories used to explain the experiences of Black, Indigenous, and Students of Colour (Solórzano & Yosso, 2002). Bell further adds that structural and institutional racism are preserved through the practices and philosophies of whiteness. Ladson-Billings (2009) echoes Bell by reiterating that racism *still* matters. She argues for the primacy of centring race in understanding many of the social relations that define life. Because critical race theory uses race as an analytic tool for understanding oppressive experiences in education, it complicates the differences between equity and equality (i.e., education debt, neoliberal racism and hegemonic whiteness). It further exposes the taken-for-granted elements of diversity and colour-blindness, where whiteness is positioned as normative, and everyone is ranked and categorised in relation to these points of opposition.

Critical race theory also has the potential to create a space for liberatory and transformative solutions to racial, gender, and class subordination. Solórzano & Yosso (2002) note that by engaging and drawing on interdisciplinary knowledge bases of Ethnic Studies, Women's Studies, Sociology, History, Humanities, and the Law to better understand the experiences of students of colour, critical race theory has the potential to flip deficit narratives by viewing personal experiences as sources of strength. Further, critical race theory draws on narratives and counternarratives that challenge a hegemonic definition of 'T'ruth, as well as traditional ideas of meritocracy, objectivity, and individualism. By drawing on storytelling, family histories, biographies, scenarios, parables, cuentos, testimonios, chronicles, and narratives, the aim of critical race theory is to interrogate master narratives and hegemonic ways of thinking about oppression and marginalisation.

Testimonio

As just one example of counternarratives within a framework of critical race theory, I highlight and look to *testimonio,* which connects action and critical self-reflexivity for transformation. *Testimonio* challenges essentialism, hegemony, and homogenisation, as every experience is valid and does not aim to represent all members of marginalised and minoritised groups (Huerta Charles, 1997). *Testimonio* also engages in discourses of solidarity in the face of ideologies of white supremacy (Villenas, 2019). One of the most important characteristics of *testimonio* is that it holds the Freirean promise of conscientization of hope, faith, and autonomy (1974, 1998). *Testimonio* upends narratives that white-wash history and its connection to current moments in time that perpetuate white supremacy and racial domination.

These stories turn upside-down the very nature of the hegemony and whiteness within educational institutions. *Testimonio* emphasises looking introspectively, talking about lived experiences, and validating individual knowledges, which, as previously discussed, are often called into question through epistemic exploitation. From these endeavours come documents, memories, and oral histories that can be used to recast and challenge pervasive theories, policies, and explanations about educational failure as a problem, not of individuals but of systemic institutionalised practices of oppression and white supremacy (Reyes and Rodrigues, 2012). As Smith et al. note, "storytelling offers a way to centre Indigenous experiences, creating a context for uncomfortable conversations and an opportunity to share our insights with readers who can connect to these ideas and push the decolonial dialogue further" (2022, p. 3).

Testimonio also adds to the evidence that challenges cosmetic diversity initiatives, wilful ignorance, as well as policies and practices that uphold a university that is undergirded by ideologies of whiteness. Significantly, *testimonio* disrupts the educational canon, challenges mainstream academic knowledge, and questions hegemonic understandings of oppression; all tenets of the liberatory potentialities of critical theory and its relationship to resistance and transformation. As the third strand of the three-prong approach, *testimonio* directly confronts the 'problem' (and its many manifestations) whilst demanding an alternative framework, lens, and tool to move forward towards education that is liberatory and transformative.

This past year I taught a course on intersectionality where I engaged critical race theory and *testimonio*. As part of the learning about *testimonio*, the class watched "*No Māori Allowed*," a documentary produced by Reikura Kahi (2023). The documentary features the story of Pukekohe, a small township in Aotearoa, New Zealand, that confronts its racist past by retelling the history of the town from a variety of members of the community. Ironically, the town's forgotten history was 'unearthed' by an American academic who wrote about the town's history of racism. This academic was subsequently criticised for telling a story that was not his own, essentially not including the stories from those who experienced it first-hand. The entirety of the process was documented by Kahi, who highlights the stories from the residents of Pukekohe, including the kaumatua (elders) who had never told their personal stories of racism in the community before, or if they did tell them, there were often not believed by the perpetrators and other members within the community. The documentary resonated deeply with the students, as it demonstrated *testimonio* in action, particularly as it relates to the way students often learn about the history of colonialism, racism, and white supremacy throughout their education in Aotearoa, New Zealand. As I discuss *testimonio* and how I bring it into the classroom community, I find it helpful to share a few reflections from the students as they relate to *testimonio* in general, as well as to the film *No Māori Allowed*, in particular. They are italicised, anonymised and peppered throughout the discussion.

> *Testimonio is not a 2D tool. It needs to be able to shift with people and their complex experiences. There is no one position or standpoint on an experience. We should avoid generalising such a thing. It cannot be a*

mode of disruption if it is only coming from one person's experience. It is a tool that needs to be used by both those who are trying to tear down the system that does not work for them, and also those within the system that are trying to make it better.

Similar to the way history is often told, or perhaps not told, is another feature of *testimonio*. *No Māori Allowed* demonstrates the power of talking back, sharing personal stories without the fear of experiencing epistemic injustice or epistemic exploitation whilst disrupting histories that are hidden and 'forgotten.' In essence, this film included all the ways that whiteness, white supremacy, and racial domination exist at the macro, micro, and individual levels.

The film, when aired to national tv, challenges the idea the New Zealand does not have significant past of racism. New Zealanders will often compare themselves to America and conclude that by comparison, racism is not an issue here. One man did it in this documentary. However, by kaumatua telling their stories this idea is challenging that segregation in Pukekohe was a bad as the Jim Crow era South. It is resistance to the idea that new Zealand is a colour blind society beyond racism. This is also the idea of critical race theory, challenging colour blindness. Critical race theory and testimonio can both be used to shed light on the racism present in New Zealand, and to resist it.

Further, as a counter-hegemonic tool of resistance, *testimonio* relies on drawing on reflexive historicity, lived experience and hidden structures, dialogic engagement with the margins, and embodiment and interdependence. Definitionally, *testimonio* is a novel or novella-length narrative told in the first person by a narrator who is also the real-life protagonist or witness of the events one recounts (Beverley, 1991). One of the most well-known examples of *testimonio* is *I, Rigoberta Menchú* (1983). Through Menchús' experiences in Guatemala, she writes her *testimonio* sharing her own experiences, how she understood her own world and life, whilst detailing the oppression and horrific events that she personally witnessed. Menchú's individual account, although undoubtedly shared by many others, is her own story and her experience as she chooses to share them. Significantly, *testimonio* rejects broad and master narratives, instead providing personal testimonies where the speaker does not speak for or represent a community, but rather performs an act of identity-formation which is simultaneously personal and collective (Yudice, 1991).

Testimonio is different from the qualitative method of in-depth interviewing, oral history narration, prose, or spoken word, as its intentional and political (Reyes and Rodriguez, 2012). What distinguishes *testimonio* from other forms of narrative, counter-stories, etc., is that the focus is most importantly *not* on 'T'ruth. In fact, Partnoy (2003) notes, the central feature of *testimonio* is neither its truth-value nor its literariness, (or lack thereof) but its ability to engender and regenerate a discourse of solidarity. As Chavez (2012) shares,

> *My stories are an attempt to recreate the instances where I collide with hegemonic ideological constructs. As an autoethnographer, my role serves to unpack the repercussions on my educational identity all along the pipeline. Exploring the development of particular identities may help inform research in understating how Latinas/os and other marginalized students of [colour] experience educational institutions in order to acquire more specific knowledge of their academic successes and failures (p. 335).*

Testimonio is a way to disrupt and challenge 'mainstream' or 'official' knowledge (Apple, 1995; Denzin, Lincoln, & Smith, 2008). Pérez Huber (2009) argues that there is an apartheid of knowledge in academia that privileges 'official knowledge' that is based on racist, sexist and Eurocentric epistemologies. Challenging the hegemony of knowledge within the academy, *testimonio* acknowledges and draws from the diverse experiences and bodies of knowledge that exist outside of academia and within Black, Indigenous and Communities of Colour. Cruz (2006) honours this point, stating that Women of Colour must begin within themselves, their families, and their experiences in order to define or examine their production of knowledges so they can tell their truths as they have experienced them.

> *The film (No Māori Allowed) broadened my understanding of tools/modes of resistance by illustrating the importance and benefits of 'by and for' knowledge and how this often does not fit into or deemed valid Eurocentric academia. It reminds me of Māori knowledge in academia, that the invalidation of indigenous knowledge perpetuates the invisibility of cultures through voicelessness. The method of testimonio allowed me to see how narratives of lived experience can be used as tools of resistance as they offer the reader an insight into how a collective phenomenon manifests as an individual's experience.*

Contemporary movements of resistance that challenge epistemically exploitative behaviours and practices are seen within such campaigns as *'Why isn't my professor Black?'* (Fereidooni et. al, 2020) *'Why isn't my professor Māori?'* (McAllister, 2019) and *'Why isn't my professor Pasifika?'* (Naepi, 2019) These campaigns of resistance challenge the whiteness of the university and the curriculum, as well as speak to the invisibility and hyper-visibility of BIPOC academics and students. Race and ethnicity are centrally located and challenge white and western forms of knowledge production. Critical race epistemologies directly interrogate and undermine the narrow foundation of knowledge that is based on a Eurocentric framework of social, historical, and cultural experiences (Delgado Bernal, 2002). Recently, the campaign *'I, too am Auckland'* (2015) brought together academics and staff from the university of Auckland in Aotearoa, New Zealand, where Māori and Pasifika members shared and exposed their experiences with racial microaggressions and epistemically exploitative behaviours. By deploying tenets of critical race theory and *testimonio*, the *'I, too, am Auckland'* campaign deliberately and purposefully exposes and undermines the white, colonial university space.

One of the most critical components of deploying *testimonio* as both a methodological and political tool is that it can be contextualised in a way that demands both the narrator and the reader understand its power and liberating potential as a form of resistance and a talking back practice within education (Cruz, 2012). Chávez reinforces this notion:

> *Testimonio* is a way to reinterpret the events we choose to depict regarding our lived experiences. Thus, while stories are many times fragmented bits and pieces of our own collective memory, these instances serve to deepen our understanding of the ways in which social relations are embedded within existing hegemonic structures— in this case, educational institutions (2012, p. 345).

Testimonio empowers the speaker or writer whilst weaving the author of the *testimonio* and the reader into a relationship that moves towards challenging hegemonic forms of thinking. *Testimonio* encourages the readers to participate and become agents of change, forging alliances with those who are at the margins (Partnoy, 2003). There must be an awareness of the relationship the *testimonio* creates between the narrator and the reader. In the case of those who are offering and sharing their stories of their educational experiences, the audience must not read these stories passively. As Cruz (2012) argues,

Testimonio demands rapt listening and its inherent intersubjectivity
when we have learned to do the kind of radical listening demanded by a
testimonialist, turning all of us who are willing to participate as listener,
storyteller, or researcher into witnesses whether we come from a place
of political solidarity or even from places of conflict" (p.463).

The *testimonio* resituates the customary manner in which stories are
shared. Within this dialogical space, *testimonio* reinforces how everyone is
simultaneously with and within the world. It engages with a dialectical
conception of consciousness, as it reinforces the interconnectivity between
educational institutions, individual and personal experiences, and how they are
all intimately intertwined with society writ large. The symbiosis between these
spaces is fluid in nature, evolving and constantly moving together. Everyone
exists in educational communities and the world simultaneously. *Testimonio*
provides a space where personal truths regarding inequities, injustices, and often
horrific experiences can come to the forefront of resistance, reinforcing the
potential for collective action and activism.

> *When I was younger, all of this was invalidated, like it never existed, and
> if it did, it wasn't that bad. In school history being told that 'you guys'
> didn't have it as bad as Australia, or the States, was completely
> invalidating, but we internalised it and believed it. So, seeing the
> testimonial of our kuia, and our tuakana in media has brought me hope,
> for my grandmother who was beaten at school, and was considered 'too
> dark' to be loved by her Pākehā mother. It brings me hope that with the
> opportunity for testimonios from the source of what happened can be
> taken seriously; I hope my grandparents can/will heal.*

hooks (1989) notes that, "it is only as allies with those who are exploited and
oppressed, working in struggles for liberation, that individuals who are not
victimised demonstrate their allegiance, their political commitment, their
determination to resist, to break with the structures of domination that offer
them personal privilege" (p.109). Through this act of testifying and witnessing,
the whiteness within the university and education (and, by extension, society)
can be disrupted, challenged, and interrogated.

Scholars and activists who are part of marginalised and minoritised
communities in Aotearoa, New Zealand have been writing about systemic racism
and whiteness in the country for quite some time, but until recently, much of the
scholarship resided within academic spaces rather than mediums where such

writing can be more accessible for a wider readership. Thus, the recently published edited volume *Towards a Grammar of Race in Aotearoa New Zealand*, Tecun, Lopesi, and Sankar (2022) is an important contribution to testimonial writing that extends beyond scholarship often reserved for the academy. This book is a compilation of chapters that foreground whiteness, racism, and settler colonialism. Each chapter provides readers with a clear understanding of the genealogy of race, whiteness in Aotearoa, New Zealand's local setting, and how they all relate to a global context. Each contributor untangles their personal experiences that are often dismissed as a one-off insult, and instead, they theorise and discuss them as personal, but also as part of a system or matrix that maintains and reproduces white supremacy. *Towards a Grammar of Race in Aotearoa New Zealand* reinforces that an individual act of racism should be seen as mutually inclusive of the institutions and structures that uphold and maintain power and whiteness.

My own interpretation of who can deploy *testimonio* within the university community coincides with the objective of *testimonio*, which is ultimately about providing an outlet for affirmative epistemological explorations (Reyes and Rodriguez (2012). *Testimonio* should not homogenise, essentialise, or dictate who can or cannot write one. There are no explicit or definitive criteria for writing and/or sharing one's own *testimonio*, other than personal experiences of subjugation and marginalisation. Another student shared;

> *I really appreciated the No Māori Allowed film, as difficult as it was to watch, and I think it really stands to affirm the power of storytelling as a form of resistance, of speaking back to dominant narratives. I think testimonio can really serve to expand critical race theory's emphasis on the importance of storytelling, and this film was a perfect example of how allowing people to tell their stories can be empowering, can be a tool of resistance, disrupting dominant stories, and can also foster a discourse of solidarity - as we saw in the documentary when the rangatahi (children) and kaumatua (elders) eventually found ways to understand each other and stand together, uplift each other, despite their vastly different lived experiences of being Māori.*

As with other forms of counternarratives and counter-stories, personal experiences carve out a space to humanise and make sense of oppressions that seem abstract to the listener and witness to the *testimonio*. Within the context of the university, the purpose of sharing one's own *testimonio*, or drawing on someone else's, is to humanise and speak back to what is often delegitimised and ignored. *Testimonio* is just one avenue in which to rupture a culture of racial microaggressions and epistemically exploitative behaviours that uphold and maintain the white university.

Significantly, *testimonio* has the potential to bridge the gap between the theoretical and abstract content of the university and the realities of society and the world writ large. It is this interconnectivity that resistance is foregrounded, as critical theory can be understood as both liberatory and action-oriented. As Huerta-Charles (2007) shares, "testimonies help me show my students how complex concepts, such as hegemony, subalternity, domination, oppression, and praxis itself, illuminate and happen in our daily actions at our schools and in our personal lives" (p.257-258). Critically reflexive practice is privileged as the site where one can learn how to turn critical thought into emancipatory action. This entails a reflexivity where one can attend to the politics of what they do and do not do at a practical level (Lather, 1991). Thus, *testimonio*, as a tool of resistance, has the potential to deliberately undermine the intersecting practices of epistemic exploitation and racial microaggressions, both of which contribute to the upholding of whiteness that is so deeply embedded within the university.

Conclusion

Teaching and learning about the insidious nature of ideologies and theories that maintain whiteness and racial domination are vital if tangible and deliberate changes are to be made. However, there is a paradox in wanting to learn, understand and challenge how white supremacy and institutional racial domination are connected to upholding an ideology of whiteness within the context of the university. On the one hand, through a deep exploration of whiteness and racism, white students and educators are tasked to move beyond a superficial understanding of such content. On the other hand, care must be taken not to centre whiteness in a way that reinforces it, but instead, work to deliberately disrupt and interrogate it. Arguably, the practice of drawing on critical race theory broadly, and *testimonio* specifically, is not something that just 'materialises' or occurs in a happenstance manner. It is vital that educators and their students collectively create a space for engaging with the discomfort that often occurs within counter-hegemonic and radical teaching and learning. Students and academics have an opportunity to complicate and interrogate ideas and experiences that can prove challenging and confrontational, yet powerful and provocative for educational and societal transformation. There must be a shared understanding of how to engage with critical theories and diverse modes of resistance in ways that have the potential to speak back and work to undermine the oppressive forces that characterise the white university. There is an intimate interconnectivity between education, dialectics, and the cognitive dissonance that often occurs when engaging with content that asks one to challenge a 'common sense' understanding of the world. It is precisely through practices like critical self-reflexivity and educating for critical consciousness, as both are instrumental when working towards rupturing an ideology of whiteness and white supremacy within and beyond the university.

PART 3

Part one (chapter 1) discussed the scaffolding and foregrounding that is cognitively and epistemologically necessary when challenging ingrained understandings of whiteness and power, and their many manifestations within and beyond education. Part one (chapter 2) situated critical theory and intersectionality as frameworks and lenses, demonstrating how one might engage critical theories that centre marginalised identities to zoom out and understand the bigger picture, ultimately paying close attention to the way that nothing can nor should be taken for granted. Part two (chapters 3-5) moved further and took a deep dive into the ways that the macro intersects with the micro, and how one can begin to understand the white university as it is upheld philosophically through the *Racial Contract, Historical Privilege, and Education Debt,* (chapter 3) through the concepts *diversity and colour-blindness* (chapter 4) and oppressive behaviours like *epistemic exploitation and racial microaggressions* (chapter 5). Significantly, chapter five also engaged education as a tool of resistance, noting how critical race theory and *testimonio* have the potential to liberate, disrupt, and transform the university. The final part and chapter of this book brings everything together, providing readers an opportunity to understand how these ideas, concepts, theories, and frameworks might be developed through university teaching and learning. What follows in chapter six is a meditation on a course I teach at my current university. The course is entitled, *Complicating Resistance: Sociology of Transformation,* and is designed in a similar way to the structure of this book. Although not a pedagogy or prescription to be replicated directly, I hope that by sharing my teaching experiences, some student feedback, and a few reflections on the course, readers may see the possibilities for resistance and transformation when working to untangle and challenge the many ways that whiteness and racial domination manifest within and beyond the university.

Chapter 6

Complicating Resistance: Teaching and Learning for Transformation

Introduction

The inspiration and motivation for writing this book is based on a third-year sociology course I have taught four times now at my current university in Aotearoa, New Zealand. The course pushes beyond a cursory learning of race and white supremacy, as it requires a commitment to sit with the cognitive dissonance that challenges hegemonic thinking and understandings of racial domination and ideologies of whiteness, both within Aotearoa, New Zealand and around the world. The chapter order of this book follows the sequence of the course, which is quite theory-heavy and asks a lot from students and professors in terms of engaging with critical self-reflexivity and educating for critical consciousness, both of which are intimately connected to learning about and interrogating theories of race and whiteness. Just as the beginning of this book foregrounds the importance of such concepts as standpoint, positionality, cultural humility, and challenging 'white talk'(among others) so too does the course I teach.

I begin this final chapter with a discussion of what needs to be resisted when imagining a different world that is free from hegemonic whiteness, racial domination, and white supremacy. I envision this world as being deeply interconnected with teaching and learning for resistance and transformation. Thus, I include a description of the course as well as an assignment that students complete after their learning of some of the concepts and theories discussed in the preceding chapters. My hope in including this final chapter is to share just one way that educators, group facilitators, and members of learning communities may consider taking the content within the book and bringing it to life.

Imagining a Better World

It is crucial for educators to recognise that resistance is a multilayered phenomenon that not only takes diverse and complex forms among students and teachers within schools but registers differently across different contexts and levels of political struggle" (Giroux, 2001, p.xxiv).

A hegemonic and white-dominated view of education frames successes and failures as individual issues, reinforcing the myth of equal opportunity and individual responsibility and accountability. Even within the most 'progressive' and liberal ideologies, the notion of false meritocracy relies so heavily on philosophies and ideas like diversity and colour-blindness that it becomes quite difficult to challenge the seeming neutrality of 'common sense,' whilst believing that the system is anything but egalitarian. This dangerous narrative is underpinned by a binary of the us vs. them mentality, cleverly crafting a story of self-defeat and blame. In other words, undermining the victim becomes a common sentiment as opposed to recognising and interrogating an uneven playing field that is framed as 'equal.'

Significantly, understanding the need to reframe education as liberatory and transformative requires close attention be paid to the external forces and outsides of school factors that must be reconceptualised. Existing social and political frameworks (subordination and domination) should not be taken for granted nor seen as mutually exclusive for a just education and world. These frameworks, which are intimately interconnected, must be challenged and resisted. Undeniably, the term resistance runs across and through the political spectrum. Within the context of the course, I argue that education that operates from a white lens and perspective must be resisted. Additionally, educational communities that uphold racial domination and subordination, both structurally and individually, must be challenged, undermined, and disrupted.

Notably, resisting these structures and practices is not a straightforward path, nor does such resistance carry a universal definition (refer back to chapter two and recognising diverse modes of resistance). Thus, I find it helpful to undergird the term resistance within my course with what Ross (2017) describes as being a *dangerous citizen*. A dangerous citizen embodies three fundamental, conjoined, and crucial generalities: political participation, critical awareness, and intentional action; all practices that coincide with critical self-reflexivity, educating for critical consciousness, and resistance. The underlying goals of being a dangerous citizen rely on understanding resistance and transformation, as well as how they are connected to disruption and disorder. Dangerous citizenship is a conceptual container for developing a radical critique of education as social control and a collection of strategies that can be used to challenge and interrogate the conforming, anti-democratic, anti-collective, and oppressive potentialities of education and society. Not surprisingly, embodying the notion of dangerous citizenship requires a commitment to moving beyond traditional means of resisting. Such engagement has the potential to rupture the status quo and challenge the hegemony of a narrative that perpetuates a 'common sense' and uncritical understanding of racial domination and whiteness. It should not be understated that the aims of embodying a 'dangerous citizen' are a direct response to an oppressive and socially unjust education and society.

Resistance further requires a commitment to challenging both the overt and institutionalised forms of oppression that are so fundamentally inherent within education and society. As Darder (2012) so eloquently states, educators and students must "create political links between the classroom, campus, and community, in ways that foster a more seamless political democratic understanding of theory and practice" (p.422). Throughout my course, I articulate the importance of understanding education as an inherently political project of resistance that aims for a democratic public life. I argue that everyone must take ownership of their political voices, engage in actions and discourses of solidarity, and strive for social change. Within this contemporary moment, there must be a commitment to wholeheartedly ground oneself within a democratic, revolutionary, and emancipatory existence.

Complicating Resistance – Sociology and Transformation

I teach at a large public university in Te Whanganui-a-Tara-(Wellington), Aotearoa, New Zealand, and am located within the sociology and social policy department. The course, *Complicating Resistance: Sociology and Transformation*, is for third-year students, and I have taught it four times since 2019. The first year I taught it, COVID-19 had been far from anything we could imagine. I was able to deploy the usual pedagogical and philosophical strategies I do for all of my classes, knowing that students would be there in person, and we would have the opportunity to connect them face to face. The second year, 2020, the course started in person, then had to move online while we were under lockdown. Luckily, I had the first three lectures uninterrupted on campus in early March, so that the 'getting to know you' component of the course had already had some time to flourish. The third year I taught the course was in 2022, when the class was taught in hybrid form, and only a few students would come in person, with masks, but the majority of the students listened in on the livestream option. Students couldn't sit next to each other, and there was very little group discussion that took place on or off-line. In 2023, I decided to submit for an exemption with my department so that this class could be held on campus, with no recordings and no livestream. Students had to be present and commit to a fully in- person teaching and learning experience. I knew this was a risky choice, as I didn't want to alienate any students who legitimately could not come to class, so I worked independently with a few students so that they could take the course and connect on zoom or facetime with a fellow student who kindly agreed to disseminate and discuss the information we learnt in class. This gave these remote students an opportunity to have small group discussions and engage the class, albeit in a different way. However, these few students fully committed to the course, so being physically present wasn't a concern I had for them.

Reflecting on these four iterations of *Complicating Resistance*, there is no surprise that the first and fourth times I taught it allowed for the full range of in-person experiences that is sorely lacking in too many university classrooms. As I have articulated throughout the previous chapters, the most meaningful and purposeful learning and reflecting is when one is in the presence of others. There is no hiding behind a screen. There is no discussion board to misinterpret what someone writes. Everyone who participates must rely on one another's body language as well as the in-person discussions so that everyone can be their full selves in the classroom community. The four times I taught this course, I have intimately seen the importance of what it means to be in the physical presence of others, learning together, working together, and thinking about transforming education and society collectively.

Each time I taught *Complicating Resistance*, there have been roughly 60 students enrolled. Like many courses within the sociology program at our university, most students self-identify as female and Pākehā/white. Within the course, there is a small number of students who self-identify as Māori, Pasifika, Southeast Asian, or South Asian, as well as other Black, Indigenous and Students of Colour, but these numbers tend to be roughly one-third of the total number of students in the course. There are also students who self-identify as mixed- race or bi-racial, the majority of whom have one parent who is European/Pākehā/white. Some students are also studying as part of an exchange from overseas universities. Additionally, there are a few students who are the first member of their family to attend university. Finally, because this is a large public university, there is a wide range of socioeconomic levels amongst the student population.

I present these demographics in a general manner to respect student anonymity and confidentiality of the students. Although the numbers are approximated, they provide a general overview of the racial, gender, and class makeup of the course. These identifiers are a vital component of how the students, tutors, and I experience the class, as together, we discuss how coming into the topics intersects with our lived experiences and particular racial standpoints and racial socialisation. I note the absence of neutrality or objectivity when considering how the critical theory we all engage with connects with our respective lives and personal experiences.

There are no prerequisites to take this course, but most students who enrol are sociology majors. I also have students from criminology, anthropology, law, and social policy, as well as other social science disciplines. Students are aware of the content and subject matter of the course per the course description, so those who enrol tend to have a commitment to the structures and requirements of the course, as well as challenging themselves with difficult discussions about race and white supremacy.

Finally, *Complicating Resistance* includes tutorials, led by the tutor, and are held once a week throughout the term. As I mentioned in the prologue, I see this course as co-led with the tutor. I have had two unbelievable tutors for the four classes, both of whom have taken the course and are not only familiar with the content, but truly understand what it means to see and understand ourselves as racialised human beings, and how this is deeply connected to making sense of the theoretical content and its relationship to action and transformation. Both of the tutors embody and understand the process of educating for critical consciousness and critical self-reflexivity, and believe in the power of critical theory being liberatory. They have been instrumental in the ways that students share their positive experiences with the course. I feel beyond lucky to have had the opportunity to work with both of them over the past few years. The success of the course is intimately connected to the time, care, and commitment of the tutors.

Complicating Resistance is a relatively new sociology course that I created to provide students with an opportunity to immerse themselves in a variety of critical theories of whiteness and race, with the objective of deliberately challenging and untangling them within and outside of the university classroom. It is an interesting course to navigate, given that many of the students who take the course may have little to no experience engaging and discussing race, racial dynamics, and whiteness outside of a colour-blind and race-evasive perspective. Thus, I am upfront with the students who take the course that the content may be brand new for some, whereas for others, the subject is one that they are quite comfortable talking about, and for others, they have intimate experiences with the content at a very person level. Within this framework, I consider how and in what capacity learning critical theories and frameworks about race and whiteness provide an opportunity to prepare students to interrogate and challenge the many facets of white supremacy both within and outside the classroom context? Connecting with the title of the course, I highlight how one might embody the notions of a dangerous citizen whilst in formal and informal learning spaces. How does learning, thinking, and action move one towards a place in which to imagine a better world where education is experienced as liberatory and transformative?

As part of the course, I ask (and continue to ask) the following questions: *What needs to change within a university classroom community to disrupt the cycle of racial domination and ideologies of whiteness and white supremacy? How can professors and students (in both predominately white and racially diverse classrooms) tangibly work within critical theoretical frameworks that aim to intangle whiteness within and beyond the university? How can and does this learning connect with diverse modes of resistance and action-oriented transformation as it relates to liberatory education?* As I consider these questions within a university teaching and learning context, I recognise that too often, whiteness and racial domination can be subversively upheld within the philosophies and pedagogies of the classroom community (through white talk and white educational discourse), ultimately reinforcing oppressive and inequitable education whilst sustaining white ignorance. Thus, I am mindful of not only what and how I teach in the classroom, but I consider, in what capacity I may be inadvertently replicating the very content I am working to undermine and dismantle. Thus, I continuously self-reflect on the entirety of the teaching and learning process throughout and beyond the course.

Creating a Dialogic and Dialectic Classroom Community

Just like the beginning of this book, there is quite a bit of scaffolding and pre-reflecting that needs to occur in a classroom community before taking a deep dive into concepts that interrogate racial domination and whiteness. Students (and their professors) must understand that no one comes to these readings, conversations, and educational spaces objectively. Everyone is part of a racialised system that relies on conformity in order to uphold and perpetuate stereotypes and hegemonic understandings of whiteness and white supremacy; specifically as it relates to education. Thus, I draw on Strmic-Pawl's (2015) critical pedagogy when teaching a class that includes both white and students of colour. Strmic-Pawl reinforces that all students must be involved within the conversation of race and whiteness by articulating how, when speaking to the larger structures of white supremacy, it becomes clear that everyone, regardless of one's race, can and does participate in the logic and hierarchy that maintains the power of whiteness. By engaging this type of critical pedagogy, I hope to create a space where everyone can pre-reflect, and continue to reflect, on some of the ways that each and every one of us is complicit within the very systems that this class is seeking to unsettle and interrogate.

The first class meeting is grounded in Watson's call to 'stay in the conversation.' Circling back to chapter one, Watson (2018) argues for creating a classroom environment that welcomes honesty, disagreement, and respect. This is imperative, as the content that I ask my students (and myself) to engage with goes beyond simplistic notions of interpreting and understanding whiteness and race. Within a 'staying in the conversation' framework, I underscore the importance of rapt listening, giving of self, and being fully present when unpacking one's own racial standpoint and racialised experiences (de Saxe, 2016; Watson, 2018). I am aware that difficult emotions may arise throughout this process, and I work to create a community that fosters a challenging yet nurturing environment. I aim to do this by deploying the tenets of cultural humility, (also discussed in chapter one), which recognises the importance of lifelong learning, institutional accountability, and critical self-reflexivity.

I find that by beginning the first class by showing a short film entitled *Cultural Humility* by Vivian Chavez, (2012),[1] students can start to see themselves as intimately part of teaching, learning, and critical self-reflexivity. The aim of the film is to break down barriers that create hostile or uncomfortable classroom environments, as students often feel that they don't know enough to contribute or are afraid to ask questions that might make them look 'unintelligent.' The film unpacks the differences between cultural humility and cultural competency, arguing that the latter leaves little to no room for ongoing learning or self-reflecting. Conversely, cultural humility creates a space to learn from one another, noting that such a practice aims for life -long learning, rethinking current assumptions and practices, as well as being open and comfortable with 'not knowing.' By showing this film, students are more willing and forthcoming to talk openly about sensitive and challenging topics, as the film frames one's understanding of the world through their respective 'funds of knowledge.'[2] In

---

[1] Link to the cultural humility film- Vivian Chavez- https://www.youtube.com/watch?v=SaSHLbS1V4w&t=20s

[2] I include the term 'funds of knowledge' as theorised by Moll et. all, 1992.

this context, funds of knowledge is what one knows, has been taught, and how one learns about the world. Cultural humility, through a funds of knowledge perspective, understands a 'lack of knowledge' as something one has not yet learnt, as opposed to seeing oneself as 'not being smart.' Thus, instead of framing this as a deficit, cultural humility sees it as something that one does not yet know, but can learn as everyone has the potential and drive to keep learning. This is vital if I am asking students to be honest and self-reflexive in their learning with both myself and the other students in the classroom community. Further, I make it a point for students to know that throughout the entirety of the course, I am continuously learning right alongside of them.

One of the most important and meaningful activities that starts off the term is something that I learnt from my time as a member of the National Coalition Building Institute (NCBI). This participatory activity, known as 'the Up/Down Exercise,' asks students (and myself) to stand or raise their hand for various identities and groups that we all belong to. We move from birth order to class status, racial and ethnic identity, learning styles and religious affiliation (among many others). Every single category is prompted with, "If you identify as XXX, please stand (or raise your hand) and be welcomed". The power of this activity is that it not only visually demonstrates the diversity within the classroom (deploying a multi-faceted understanding of the term) but also welcomes everyone to the classroom space for who they are and all that they embody. It also serves to complicate visual representation of how we identify, as this helps students flesh out and work to better understand terms like colour-blindness, diversity, whiteness, and race. In fact, when teaching these concepts, we often circle back to the Up/Down activity, noting how colourism and the social construction of race and whiteness connect with how we understand ours and others' racialised selves. Given the content that we work through during the term, this activity reinforces that we all bring our multiple and varied identities, as well as our own standpoints and positionalities, to the readings, class discussions, and assessment tasks. Students have also shared that this activity affirms them as full human beings. Most important, it creates a space to have challenging conversations, knowing all of us are so much more than the way we are stereotyped, perceived and ascribed within society.

I also frontload the theory-content lectures with terms such as double consciousness (duBois), double image, (Seidl and Hancock), critical self-reflexivity, and educating for critical consciousness (Freire), noting how, when committing to this course, students will be able to see the potentialities of critical theory and its relationship to unlearning, re-learning, and action. I remind students how vital it is that the levels of hierarchy that often plague academia come down throughout such learning, discussions, and personal growth. My students must know that I, too, engage in the honest and critical self-reflecting that I am asking of them. If I do not participate in such learning with my students, how can I ask them to do the same?

Like the blurred lines between theory and practice, self-reflexivity and the commitment to difficult conversations do not only happen within the bounds of the university, nor are they definitive acts. I continuously remind students that developing a racial consciousness is a lifelong process. Challenging whiteness and racial injustice through acts such as attending marches, posting on social media and taking courses on race and racism, though part of a larger movement towards anti-racism and challenging white supremacy, can in themselves be seen as performative or self-congratulatory. I urge students to keep this in mind when learning about critical theories of race and whiteness, asking them to pay close attention to how centring their own whiteness is very different to putting whiteness in the centre, with deliberate attention paid to interrogating and challenging it. In other words, while they may work to understand how their whiteness has enabled them to be complicit in upholding racist structures, they must seek to challenge their whiteness by confronting it in a way that doesn't turn the attention back to them. This is not an easy task, but I encourage students (particularly white and Pākehā students) to see themselves as listeners first, being careful to note when it is appropriate for them to speak and when it isn't. Not surprisingly, this is a topic that we discuss quite often throughout the term.

The content I teach in this course also follows the content and chapter order of this book. Each class session engages with a particular critical theory or concept, which I then ask students to think about in terms of what it might mean to 'humanise' the theories. I often bring in videos, podcasts, and guest lecturers, all of which provide a variety of opportunities and mediums for students to understand the terms, both conceptually and how they manifest in education and society. As mentioned in earlier chapters, I ask students to write a reflection after each lecture, focusing on how they connect to the concept or theory, as well as how they experience the concept personally or if they have lived most of their life removed from having to think too deeply about the concept. These reflections are pedagogically significant as I can gauge students' understanding of the concepts and theories. They also provide me with an opportunity to see how students become and continue to be racially socialised and what this means in regard to their relationship with education. Each class is different from the one prior, which confirms the importance I put on getting to know all of my students as full human beings throughout the entirety of the course. I try to meet with each student in person (either in my office or at a café on campus) during the first month of the course. These are very low-stakes meetings, as they are designed to get to know the students outside of the classroom setting. The majority of the students share that I am the first professor they have ever met outside of class. I am not surprised by this statement, but I see it as emblematic of our current culture of distance and individual responsibility in university courses. I attempt to push against this philosophy throughout the entirety of the course.

After I spend roughly six weeks engaging in the teaching and learning of the critical theory, I assign the first assignment; a Racial Autobiography. What follows is a discussion of the assignment, as well as my hope for how it provides students an opportunity to apply the critical theory to personal experiences, and how this is directly connected to critical self-reflexivity, educating for critical consciousness and action.

Racial Autobiography[3]

The racial autobiography assignment is due after the first six lectures on critical theories of race and whiteness. I borrow Watson's (2018) version of a Racial Autobiography that she assigns to her teacher education students. Watson states, "who we are influences how we form relationships and understand others. In this assignment, I hope you will learn more about your beliefs and assumptions, where these assumptions come from, and how these assumptions may influence your behaviour" (p.42). Although the assignment is called a 'Racial Autobiography,' students who choose to write their story in a way that draws on the characteristics of *testimonio* may choose to title it that instead. They share that titling the assignment their *testimonio* gave them an opportunity to write in a way that feels more like talking-back whilst sharing their experience so others can read with the perspective of engaging in a discourse of solidarity. I refer to Cruz (2012), who reinforces the purpose and power of *testimonio* in education. She argues:

> *Testimonio* demands rapt listening and its inherent intersubjectivity when we have learned to do the kind of radical listening demanded by a testimonialist, turning all of us who are willing to participate as listener,

---

[3] Elements of this section are drawn from de Saxe & Ker (2023).

storyteller, or researcher into witnesses whether we come from a place of political solidarity or even from places of conflict (p.463).

To reiterate, *testimonio* resituates the customary way stories are shared. The traditional structures and dominant paradigms of education are called into question, and the ones commonly at the margins move to the front. These stories turn upside-down the very nature of the hegemony of our educational institutions. Thus, whether students choose to call this assignment their *testimonio* or a 'Racial Autobiography,' both engage in a writing exercise that asks them to self-reflect, drawing on critical theory, ultimately moving beyond the traditional forms of sharing their learning and understanding of the course content as it connects to their lives.

The assignment is broken up into two parts: 1) students critically self-reflect upon a particular experience and/or moment in their lives where they think about race (either directly or indirectly); and 2) students analyse this moment through the theoretical lens and frameworks of an epistemology of white ignorance (Applebaum, 2019; Mills 2007) and the Racial Contract (Mills, 2007). Although they have learnt quite a few other theories, these two tend to allow students an opportunity to participate in a way of thinking and writing that supports a depth vs. breadth approach to learning and reflecting. To reiterate, the importance of reflecting upon one's standpoint and positionality is so that students can see how interconnected and contextually specific they are when challenging knowledge, power and hegemonic thinking and learning. Another component of this assignment is that students bring a hard copy with them to the lecture, where they then meet in small groups (no more than 2 or 3) to read their essays out loud to one another. This is not common practice in university classrooms, but over the years, I have found it quite a powerful exercise, as the listener is in the presence of the story and storyteller, thus being asked to engage in active listening and learning. What follows are some of the observations and analyses from all four cohorts of students and their racial autobiography and *testimonio* assignments.

Unpacking the Racial Autobiography

Reflecting on their racial autobiographies, I ask students to think of a moment in their lives when they considered race. For example, *What ideas did you grow up with regarding race? What is the most important image you've seen, or encounter you've had, regarding race? What was your first awareness of your race or ethnicity? How does your experience with race connect with your relationship to education?* After four iterations of this assignment, I observe some commonalities within students' chosen moments and how they apply their racial standpoint and experience within systems that uphold, maintain, and reinforce racial stratification and the privileging of whiteness.

Several students reflect upon their experiences of learning through a Pākehā-centric education system in Aotearoa. The different ways Māori and Pākehā students navigate these tensions of living in a settler-colonial country that centres colonial narratives, yet has an obligation to honour Te Tiriti o Waitangi, and specifically in their racial autobiographies, indicating their ongoing journeys of understanding their racialised selves situating in their educational environments. For some students, this was the first time they are asked to consider the operation of race and whiteness in their education, whereas, for other students, their racial awareness has always informed how they understand and navigate education.

Some of the international students in the class share how the Racial Contract and epistemology of white ignorance operationalise within their home countries. For example, a few students from southeast Asia write about their experience of linking theoretical frameworks into a southeast Asian context. As discussed throughout the term, the way whiteness manifests is content, geographically, historically, and politically specific. Upon reflecting throughout their racial autobiographies, students note that after considering the tenets that characterise the Racial Contract, (hegemony, coded language, stereotypes, etc.), they can see how they might deploy such frameworks to help make sense of and challenge the maintenance of hierarchy and marginalisation in their home countries.

In regard to thinking about how the spatial contract operates within the Racial Contract, a few Māori and Pasifika students talk about their experiences of feeling out of place, unwelcome, and discriminated against in certain spaces. In contrast, white and Pākehā students come to see and understand how they are welcomed into all spaces without any question, thus demonstrating how whiteness is normalised and universalised as belonging everywhere and anywhere. Although confronting, students articulate how they see these theories 'come to life' within their daily, often seemingly mundane experiences.

Some students also chose to reflect upon their university application experience, initially understanding their acceptance or rejection purely based on an individual system of merit and hard work. However, after unpacking their narrative within an epistemology of white ignorance, they come to understand how the system is designed and maintained within a structure of normalising and privileging whiteness as it relates to 'success'. During this process, students begin to make sense of how their racial standpoints, personal narratives, and actions either uphold or challenge power. Throughout this process, students grapple with the ways subjectivity is bound to the structural, and therefore holds the potential for transformation.

My observations also suggest that Pākehā/white and Black, Indigenous, and Students of Colour can connect with an epistemology of white ignorance and the Racial Contract, albeit in different ways. For example, many BIPOC students recognise that what they personally experience is legitimised through a theoretical framework of white ignorance, which echoes hooks' (1994) notion that theory is liberatory. For example, by drawing on critical theories of race, students see and consider the ways they have been systematically disadvantaged and marginalised because of their racial identity. Additionally, students discuss that by having the freedom to consider themselves in a racialised light, they are better able to reflect and legitimise thoughts they have always had.

Conversely, for many Pākehā/white students, learning about an epistemology of white ignorance and the Racial Contract provides them with tools to better understand previously unexamined behaviours. Students reveal that by not recognising their white racial identity, they absolve themselves as racial beings, essentially upholding and normalising whiteness. They also come to see and recognise that their perceived absence of race is, in fact, a racial experience. This process can be quite confronting for white students as it opens up a space to think about how and why their actions reinforce and normalise structures of whiteness, so that they can work towards exposing and undermining them within their own lives. Ultimately, I hope that the process allows white students to develop a more nuanced perspective on whiteness, noting how this has enabled access to certain aspects of society—how students both see their own, and how other people view their white racial identity.

For the Black, Indigenous and Students of Colour in the course, they share how their engagement with these concepts has been one of the first times in their university learning where critical theory speaks directly to their personal experiences around race and racism. Students articulate that prior to learning about the Racial Contract and epistemology of ignorance, they believed their experiences were something that was understood anecdotally, without any connection to academia or theory. Students also share that having these terms that speak to their experiences validates the importance of centring their reality within their university learning. This reflecting underscores hooks' (1994) claim that critical theory can be both liberatory and emancipatory. The power of the racial autobiography assignment and its inclusion of critical theory is that it meets students where they are at, so the concepts resonate and speak directly to lived experiences and one's personal relationship to race and whiteness based on these experiences.

Towards a Co-Conspiratorial Framework

Solidarity can never be expressed by hearing someone's pain and then turning the conversation back to yourself. Solidarity means trying to understand the ways our communities experience unique forms of oppression and marginalisation. It means showing up for one another to bear witness and then expanding our fight to include the challenges faced by other communities besides our own (Garza, 2020).

Revisiting the purpose of this course, (and, by extension, this book), most white university students have few experiences in university settings where they can spend a significant amount of time talking and learning about whiteness and white supremacy. For those who have immersed themselves in such content, feelings of guilt, shame, and anger often emerge, as such discussions can be solely focused on historical acts, individual behaviours, and disconnected experiences. Notably, Maddison (2011, as cited within Norris, 2019) argues for the importance of distinguishing healthy white guilt from unhealthy white guilt, as the former can lead to action and transformation, while the latter often results in paralysis. As students reflected on their racial autobiographies, it became apparent that many found the process therapeutic, cathartic, yet startling and confronting; it pushed them to think about issues they had not thought of previously, or that they had chosen not to think about as it was too confronting and uncomfortable. At the same time, many viewed the assignment as a catalyst for an ongoing process of (un)learning and challenging whiteness. The assignment gave white and Pākehā students a way to talk to their family and friends about race and whiteness, as well as unpack the assumptions, experiences, and ideas they had previously held about their education and identities.

Part of the process of activating critical self-reflexivity through a theoretical framework of the Racial Contract and an epistemology of white ignorance asks students to see how their learning can contribute to breaking the stronghold that ideologies of whiteness and racial domination have upon education and society. Many students express their frustration with questioning what they can 'do' with this knowledge and how it has the potential to overtly challenge racism. Drawing on the tenets of educating for critical consciousness and its relationship to action, I share with students an idea known as 'co-conspirator' (Garza, 2020). Notably, embodying the tenets of a co-conspirator intersects well with the characteristics of dangerous citizenship. In fact, when understood together, the potential for connecting teaching, learning, and action straddle both ideas.

Co-conspirator is a concept that recognises that dismantling racist structures requires white people to de-centre whiteness and fight with Black, Indigenous, and Communities of Colour towards racial justice, rather than supporting them from the 'side-lines' as the term allyship often suggests (Knittel, 2018; C-Span, 2019). There is growing consensus among BIPOC activists that allyship, both as an action and an identity, has become largely performative; as Kluttz, Walker and Walter (2020) argue, dominant discourses of allyship "lull[s] us into a false notion of having 'achieved' a status that does not invite continued questioning and constant un-settling" (p. 53). Consequently, the power to achieve sustained, structural transformation through acts of allyship become lost (Petersen-Smith & Bean, 2015). This notion is best summarized by Black Lives Matter co-founder, Alicia Garza (Move to End Violence, 2016), who states:

> Co-conspiracy is about what we do in action, not just in language. It is about moving through guilt and shame and recognizing that we did not create none of this stuff. And so what we are taking responsibility for is the power that we hold to transform our conditions. (para. 5)

A central aim of being a co-conspirator is to continually disrupt the cycle of white ignorance that enables whiteness to remain invisible. It is important for white students and professors to understand the (un)learning that happens within the classroom not as a way of achieving an ally identity, but rather, to perceive the university as a space to begin and reiterate processes of challenging white ignorance and their connection to sustained racial domination within and beyond educational institutions. Solidarity and co-conspiratorial work consider the following question as it relates to the power of whiteness and white supremacy: *What might we do to strengthen the basis of alliance between marginalised communities when there is too narrow an understanding of what issues impact whom?* As Garza argues, we must be diligent about building alliances that have depth and rigour. Shallow unity will always fall apart under pressure (2020).

The pedagogy and philosophy of the course are driven by a co-conspiratorial and dangerous citizenship lens and framework. The premise of learning to unlearn, as well as the interconnecting of critical self-reflexivity, educating for critical consciousness, and critical theory, all serve as ways to better understand one's connection to race and whiteness, and the potential to challenge, resist, and transform. *Complicating Resistance* reinforces the importance of paying attention to, and staying with the feelings of discomfort. The course also asks quite a lot from students in terms of their commitment to the content and to each other. I also recognise and consider my own privilege in being able to speak and teach about this content with fewer ramifications and risks as they relate to epistemic injustice (Fricker, 2007). Further, I realise the limits to what I can and cannot speak about when reflecting on and challenging white supremacy and racial domination. With this in mind, I envision a co-conspiratorial framework as something that has the potential to create a space for actively undermining the power imbalances and racist structures that are too often upheld rather than directly confronted and challenged.

The processes of interrogating and untangling whiteness in the classroom should not be confined to a binary academia/activist framework, but instead, located at the intersections of identity, physical, and intellectual spaces throughout society, including within and beyond the university. The iterative skills students and professors build through embodying a co-conspiratorial role within the classroom community enable a shared understanding that the various pedagogical and activist spaces they move through are inextricably linked and in constant dialogue with each other. This racial autobiography assignment is just one way that students may learn to develop a deeper and more nuanced understanding of whiteness and race, working to expose and challenge white ignorance within education and society.

Conclusion

I hope that through applying theories such as an epistemology of white ignorance and the Racial Contract (among others discussed throughout the book and the course) to lived experiences, students and professors may see the potentialities that can arise from critically self-reflecting on their experiences of being racialised and socialised, as well as how these experiences connect to how they live their lives. It is, therefore, the responsibility of professors, students, and members of educational communities to provide ways of undermining and interrogating racial domination, whiteness, and white supremacy.

In fact, one of the most important components of this course is for students to understand that their learning must move beyond the walls of the university classroom community. One of the first discussions we have as a class is for students to consider how they might take the content from the course and 'pay it forward.' I often talk with the students about rephrasing some of the concepts for someone who isn't able to spend hours a week reading, discussing, and reflecting on the topics we engage; both theoretically and how they manifest in one's own life and community. I ask students to consider some of the ways they might partake in challenging conversations with family and friends that, before taking the course, they had previously avoided. In fact, the bridging of the theory and one's personal relationship to the theory is what distinguishes the learning in the class from other courses. I share just a few comments from students over the years after they completed the course and have since moved on from university:

Overall, this course has made me realise a lot of things 'taken for granted' are actually imposed mechanisms that perpetuate these systems of power. Therefore, in order to begin working against them, you almost have to be hyper-aware and constantly question your line of thinking and those around you. Or at least this course has made me hyper-aware, and I can now associate the concepts learnt to moments and aspects of my life.

To be honest, I feel this course has truly given me the building blocks to understand and engage in conversations regarding these topics. There have been many things I could not explain before coming into this course, however with the help of these lectures, I have been able to understand and become more aware. Learning about proximity to whiteness is prime example of an eye opener for me.

My grandmother doesn't engage with her Māori community because of her experiences in childhood, she doesn't interact with social institutions because of her experiences with education. She is a perfect example of someone whose intersections consequently compounded themselves to become what I would call a social blind spot, someone so marginalised she would never frequent any social spaces, a person not considered, seen or heard but a person who needs it most. This realisation helped me to understand the basic message of this class, and in seeing her I was able to see others and think further than just race but deeper into who we are speaking for and in our stand to speak, are we truly speaking for our community or just ourselves and those alike.

It is a precarious and tense time to teach within the university. The disruption of covid has left many of classrooms empty, as students depend (for good reasons) on recordings and distance learning. This has had a serious impact on students' and professors' ability to physically be in the presence of others. What happens when one is both complacent and complicit in conceptualising teaching, learning, and self-reflexivity as an individual rather than a collective endeavour? How can one push against this narrative and challenge what is moving towards an accepted system where courses serve as merely something one needs for degree completion rather than learning for the sake of learning? Unfortunately, this is the reality for many within university communities. I have had to adapt the teaching of this course since the first time I taught it in 2019. I frequently remind myself of the purpose and philosophy of the course, which asks students to identify and challenge racism and white supremacy, recognising the need for a comprehensive understanding of the explicit and implicit ways that unexamined whiteness reinforces the inherent oppression found within educational institutions and communities. I hope to continuously work towards embodying the ethos of a dangerous citizen and being a co-conspirator, knowing that collectively, there is an opportunity and potential to interrupt whiteness through liberatory education and resistance.

Conclusion

I started this book contextualising the precarious nature of universities, discussing how teaching feels more constrained, restricted, and, in many cases, more stressful given the distractions and the difficult realities that many students experience in their lives outside of the university. However, within the current context, it is imperative for academics to recognise how and in what compacity whiteness is reinforced and privileged as the norm and status quo. If whiteness isn't actively challenged and interrogated (in its many manifestations), it will continue to be replicated both within and outside of our educational institutions. It is necessity to understand that interrupting the many dimensions of race and whiteness needs to extend beyond one course, workshop, or reading a book or two. These are all part of a lifelong process of learning, reflection, and action. Teaching and learning are intimately connected to how one understand themselves as racialised beings, and that this understanding has the potential to lead to a place of recognising the mutual inclusivity of what counts as 'knowledge,' why one believes what they do, and how one's current understandings of the world are not fixed, but rather undetermined. I hope that all educators can see themselves as learning alongside their students, aiming to challenge the status quo of hegemony that sees whiteness as 'normal,' as well as how the university upholds and maintains white supremacy. My goal throughout this book is to demonstrate that universities can be both sites to resist and sites of resistance. I hold onto the vision that another world is possible, where students and professors can engage in learning for the sake of learning, believing that the content brought into the classroom presents an opportunity to share it with others outside of the university context. I wholeheartedly believe that minds can be changed, epistemologies can be challenged, and education can be the practice of true human freedom.

I end this book by drawing on Medina's (2019) concept of epistemic activism. Medina understands epistemic activism as waking people up from their epistemic slumbers, calling attention to how they are complicit with vulnerabilities to patterns of racial violence and how they can disrupt their complicity. Epistemic activism is about reorienting the way one understands and experiences the world. It requires a realisation that no one is an empty vessel to be filled with knowledge, as all knowledge is someone's 'T'ruth. What this book has argued is that this 'T'ruth is often drawn from white, western, colonial, heteronormative, ableist and patriarchal perspectives. What happens if one allows themself to untangle the many ways that they have been taught and socialised to understand such 'T'ruth? What potentialities may arise when taking the time out of plugged-in lives to be present and immerse oneself in teaching and learning that provides opportunities to unlearn so as to challenge and interrupt the stronghold that whiteness has upon ones' mind and body?

The final class meeting of the *Complicating Resistance* course was in mid-2023. We all gathered around to have some final thoughts about our time together. I wrote this book to honour the time and care my students have put into their learning. It is a commitment and a process that is also a privilege. We must use this privilege as educators to work and learn with students, knowing that they are the next generation who have the potential to make this world better than it is now. I end with another quote from bell hooks and her seminal book *Teaching to Transgress: Education as the Practice of Freedom*. It is a quote from chapter four, where she writes a dialogue between herself, Gloria Jean Watson, conversing with her pen name, bell hooks, about Paulo Freire. hooks quotes Freire when she reflects on how a privileged critical thinker can approach the sharing of knowledge and resources with those who are in need:

> Authentic help means that all who are involved help each other mutually, growing together in the common effort to understand the reality which they seek to transform. Only through such praxis-in which those who help and those who are being helped help each other simultaneously- can the act of helping become free from the distortion in which the helper dominates the helped (Freire as cited within hooks, 1994, p. 54).

References

Aanerud, R. (2015) Humility and whiteness: "How did I look without seeing, hear without listening?" pp. 101-115. In Yancy, G. (2015). *White self-criticality beyond anti-racism: How does it feel to be a white problem?* Lexington Books: New York.

Ahmed, S. (2017). *Living a feminist life.* Durham and London: Duke University Press.

Ahmed, S. (2012). *On being included: Racism and diversity in institutional life.* Durham and London: Duke University Press.

Ambikaipaker, M. (2019). Everyday political whiteness and diversity university. *Kalfou.* 6(2). 269-279.

Andres, K (2018). *The Black studies movement in Britain: Racism, Whiteness and Decolonising the Academy.* pp. 271-287. In Arday, J. and Mirza (H.S. (eds). *Dismantling race in higher education.* Palgrave.

Annamma, Subini Ancy, Beth A. Ferri, and David .J Connor. 2018. "Disability Critical Race Theory: Exploring the Intersectional Lineage, Emergence, and Potential Futures of DisCrit in Education." Review of Research in Education 42(2018): 46-71. http://www.jstor.org/stable/44668713.

Anyon, J. (2011). *Marx and education.* New York: Routledge.

Anyon, J. (2005). *Radical possibilities: Public policy, urban education, and a new social movement.* New York: Routledge.

Anyon, J. (1994). The retreat of Marxism and socialist feminism: Postmodern and poststructural theories in education. *Curriculum Inquiry.* 2 (2). 115-133.

Anzáldua, G. (1997). La conciencia de la mestiza: Towards a new consciousness. In A.M.Garcia, *Chicana feminist thought: The basic historical writings* (pp.270-274). New York: Routledge.

Anzáldua, G. (1987). *Borderlands/ la frontera: the new mestiza.* San Francisco: Aunt Lute Book Company.

Apple, M.W. (2008). Can schooling contribute to a more just society? *Education, citizenship, and social justice.* 3(3), pp. 239-261.

Apple, M. W. & Beane, J. A. (2007). *Democratic schools.* Virginia: Association for supervision and curriculum and development.

Apple, M. W., & Buras, K. (2006). *The subaltern speak: Curriculum, power, and educational struggles.* New York, NY: Routledge.

Apple, M.W. (1995). *Education and power: Second edition.* New York and London: Routledge.

Apple, M.W. (1983). The politics of official knowledge: Does a national curriculum make sense? *Teachers College Record.* 95(2), 222-241.

Applebaum, B. (2021). *White educators negotiating complicity: Roadblocks paved with good intentions.* Lexington Books: New York.

Applebaum, B. (2019). White ignorance, epistemic injustice and the challenges of teaching for critical social consciousness. In Yancy, G. (Ed.) (2019) *Educating for critical consciousness* (pp. 28-44). New York: Routledge.

Applebaum, B. (2018). Listen! Microaggressions, epistemic injustice and *whose* minds are being coddled? *Philosophy of education.* pp 190-201.

Applebaum, B. (2015). Flipping the script... and still a problem. *Staying in the anxiety of being a problem.* In Yancy. G. (2015). *White self-criticality beyond anti-racism: How does it feel to be a white problem?* Lanham: Lexington Books.

Arday, J., & Mirza, H. S. (2018). *Dismantling Race in Higher Education: Racism, Whiteness and Decolonising the Academy.* Springer International Publishing AG. https://doi.org/10.1007/978-3-319-60261-5

Au, W. (2012). *Critical curriculum studies: Education,* consciousness *and the politics of knowing.* New York: Routledge.

Awatere, D. (1984). *Māori sovereignty.* Broadsheet.

Ayers, R. & Ayers, W. (2011). *Teaching the taboo: Courage and imagination in the classroom.* New York and London: Teachers College Press.

Azarmandi, M. (2022). The limits of Pākehā treaty work: Why race matters to anti-racism. In Tecun, A., Lopesi, L. & Sankar, A. (2022). *Towards a grammar of race in Aotearoa New Zealand.* (pp. 138-150). Wellington: Bridget Williams Books.

Bailey, A. (2105). "White talk" as a barrier to understanding the problem with whiteness. Pp. 37-57. In Yancy, G. (2015). *White self-criticality beyond anti-racism: How does it feel to be a white problem?* Lexington Books: New York.

Bargh, M. (2007). *Resistance: An indigenous response to neoliberalism.* Wellington: Huia.

Beaman, J. & Petts, A. (2020). Towards a global theory of colorblindness: Comparing Color- blind racial ideology in France and the United States. *Sociology Compass.* https:doilorg/10.111/soc4.12774.

Bécares, L., Cormack, D., & Harris, R. (2013). Ethnic density and area deprivation: Neighbourhood effects on Māori health and racial discrimination in Aotearoa/New Zealand. *Social Science and Medicine, 88,* 76-82.

Bell, A. (2020). Reverberating historical privilege of a "middling" sort of settler family. *Geneology.* 4(46).

Berenstain, N. (2016). Epistemic exploitation. *Ergo* 3(22):569–590.

Berry, T.R. (2010). Engaged pedagogy and critical race feminism. *Educational Foundations.* Summer-Fall. 19-26.

Beverley, J. (1991). "Through all things modern": Second thoughts on testimonio. *Boundary,* 2(18), 1-21.

Biesta, G. J. J. (2006). *Beyond learning: Democratic education for a human future.* Boulder, CO: Paradigm Publishers.

Binney, J. (2012). *Redemption songs: A life of Te Kooti Arikirangi Te Turuki.* Bridget Williams Books.

Bishop, R., Berryman, M., Tiakiwai, S., & Richardson, C. (2003). *Te Kōtahitanga: The experiences of year 9 and 10 Māori students in mainstream classrooms: Report to the Ministry of Education.* New Zealand: Ministry of Education.

Bonilla-Silva, E. (2015). The structure of racism in color-blind, "post-racial" America. *American Behavioral Scientists.* 59(11). Pp 1358-1376.

Bonilla-Silva, E. (2003). "New racism," color-blind racism, and the future. In A.W. Doane & E. Bonilla-Silva (Eds.). *White out: The continuing significance of racism.* pp 271-284. New York: Routledge.

Borell, B., Moewaka Barnes, H., & McCreanor, T. (2018). Conceptualising historical privilege: The flip side of historical trauma, a brief examination. *AlterNative: An International Journal of Indigenous Peoples, 14*(1), 25-34.

Brunsma, D. L., Brown, E. S., & Placier, P. (2012). Teaching race at historically white colleges and Universities: Identifying and dismantling the walls of whiteness. *Critical Sociology, 39*(5), 717-738.

Burke M.A. (2017). Colorblind racism: Identities, ideologies, and shifting subjectivities. *Sociological Perspectives.* 60(5) pp. 857-865.

Came-Friar, H., McCreanor, T., Manson, L., & Nuku, K. (2019). Upholding Te Tiriti, ending institutional racism and Crown inaction on health equity. *New Zealand Medical Journal, 132*(1492), 62-66.

Chávez, M.S. (2012): Autoethnography; a Chicana's methodological research tool: The role of storytelling for those who have no choice but to do critical race theory. *Equity and Excellence in Education, 45*(2),334-348.

Chavez, V. (2012). *Cultural humility.* "Film." Creativecommons.

Coaston, Intersectionality, explained: meet Kimberlé Crenshaw, who coined the term – Vox (2019). Available at: https://www.vox.com/the-highlight/2019/5/20/18542843/intersectionality-conservatism-law-race-gender-discrimination.

Collins, P. H. & Bilge, S. (2016). *Intersectionality.* Cambridge: Polity Press.

Collins, P. H. (2000). *Black feminist thought: Knowledge, consciousness, and the politics of empowerment* (Revised ed.). New York: Routledge.

Connell, R. (2007). *Southern theory: The global dynamics of knowledge in social science.* Massachusetts: Polity Press.

Code, L. (1990). *What can she know? Feminist theory and the construction of knowledge.* Ithaca: Cornell University Press.

C-Span (2019, March 19). We Want to Do More Than Survive. [Video file]. Retrieved from https://www.c-span.org/video/?458837-1/we-survive

Cruz, C. (2012). Making curriculum from scratch: Testimonio in an urban classroom. *Equity & Excellence in Education, 45*(3), 460-471.

Cruz, C. (2006). *Toward an epistemology of a brown body.* In Chicana/Latina education in everyday life. Feminist perspectives on pedagogy and epistemology (pp.59-79). New York: State University of New York Press.

Dadds, J.H. (2011). Feminisms: Embodying the critical. In Levinson, B.A.U. *Beyond critique: Exploring critical social theories and education* (pp. 171–196). Boulder: Paradigm Publishers.

Darder, A. (2012). Neoliberalism in the Academic Borderlands: An On-going Struggle for Equality and Human Rights. *Educational Studies, 48*(5), 412-426

Davies, B., & Bansel, P. (2007). Neoliberalism and education. *International Journal of Qualitative Studies in Education, 20*(3), 247-259.

de Saxe, J.G. & Ker, A. (2023). Disrupting an Epistemology of White Ignorance through writing a Racial Autobiography. *Critical Education.* 14(2). Pp.86-100. (equally shared nature and scale of contribution).

de Saxe, J.G. (2022). Unsettling the "White University" Undermining Color-blindness through Critical Race Theory and Testimonio. *Journal for Critical Education and Policy Studies.* 19(3). Pp 196-223.

de Saxe. (2021). Unpacking and interrogating White supremacy educating for critical consciousness and praxis. *Whiteness and Education (Print), 6*(1), 60–74. https://doi.org/10.1080/23793406.2021.1893611

de Saxe, J.G. and Trotter-Simons, B.E. (2021). Intersectionality, Decolonisation and Educating for Critical Consciousness: Rethinking Praxis and Resistance in Education. *Journal of Thought.* 55(1/2 Spring/Summer).pp 3-20. (equally shared nature and scale of contribution).

de Saxe, J.G. (2019). Complicating Resistance: Intersectionality, Liberation, and Democracy. Pp. 127-145. In Yancy, G. (2019) *Educating for Critical Consciousness in the Age of Trump.* Routledge: New York. In Yancy, G. (2019) *Educating for Critical Consciousness in the Age of Trump.* Routledge: New York.

de Saxe, J.G. & Gourd, T. (2019). *Radical educators: Rearticulating education and social change: Teacher agency and resistance, early 20th Century to the present.* New York: Routledge.

de Saxe, J.G. (2016). *Critical feminism and critical education. An interdisciplinary approach to teacher education.* Routledge: New York.

Delgado Bernal, D. (2002). Critical race theory, Latino critical theory, and critical race-gendered epistemologies: Recognizing students of color as holders and creators of knowledge. *Qualitative Inquiry,* 8(1), 105-126.

Denzin, N.K., Lincoln, Y.S., Smith, L.T. (2008). *Handbook of critical and indigenous methodologies.* Los Angeles: Sage Publications.

Dhillon, J. (2017). Feminism must be lived: An interview with Sara Ahmed. Retreived from truthout.org.

DiAngelo, R. 2012. What makes Racism so hard for whites to see?" *Counterpoints* 398: pp. 167–189.

Doane, A. (2017). Beyond color-blindness: (Re) theorizing racial ideology. *Sociological Perspectives.* 60 (5). Pp.975-991.

Dotson, K. (2014). Conceptualizing epistemic oppression. *Social epistemology,* 28 (2). pp. 115-138.

Dotson, K. (2011). Tracking epistemic violence, tracking practices of silencing. *Hypatia.* 26 (2). pp. 236-257.

Du Bois, W.E.B. (1903, 1994). *The souls of black folk.* Mineola, New York: Dover Publications, Inc.

Duina, F. 2018. *Broke and Patriotic: Why Poor Americans Love Their Country.* Stanford, CA: Stanford University Press.

Dunne, G. & Kotsonis, A. (2023). Epistemic exploitation in education. *Educational Philosophy and Theory,* 55(3). Pp 343-355.

Eddo-Lodge, R. (2017). *Why I'm no longer talking to white people about race.* London: Bloomsbury Publishing.

Elers, C. H., & Jayan, P. (2020). "This is us": Free speech embedded in whiteness, racism and coloniality in Aotearoa, New Zealand. *First Amendment Studies,* 54(2), 236-249.

Embrick, D. G., & Moore, W. L. (2020). White Space(s) and the Reproduction of White Supremacy. *American Behavioral Scientist,* 64(14), 1935–1945. https://doi.org/10.1177/0002764220975053

Evans, E. (2016). Intersectionality as feminist praxis in the UK. *Women's Studies International Forum,* 59, pp. 67–75.

Fanon, F. (1967). *Black skin, White masks.* New York: Grove.

Fereidooni, K., Thompson, V. E., & Kessé, E. N. (2020). Why isn't my professor black?: A roundtable. In *Locating African European Studies* (1st ed., Vol. 1, pp. 247–256). Routledge. https://doi.org/10.4324/9780429491092-18

Fillion Wilson, M.A. (2019). Teaching whiteness in the neoliberal university: Positionality, privilege, resistance and transformation. In Bolton, P., Smith, C., & Bebout, L. (Eds.). *Teaching with tension: Race, resistance, and reality in the classroom.* (pp. 217-235). Evanston, Illinois: Northwestern University Press.

Foste, Z. (2020). Remaining vigilant: reflexive considerations for white researchers studying whiteness. *Whiteness and education.* 5(2) pp. 131-146.

Freire, P. (1998). *Pedagogy of freedom: Ethics, democracy, and civic courage.* Lanham, Maryland: Rowman & Littlefield.

Freire, P. (1974). *Education for critical consciousness.* New York: The Continuum International Publishing Group.

Freire, P. (1970). *The pedagogy of the oppressed.* New York: The continuum International publishing group.

Fricker, M. (2007). *Epistemic injustice: Power and the ethics of knowing.* Oxford: Oxford University Press.

Garza, A. (2020). *The purpose of power: How to build movements for the 21st century.* United Kingdom: Random House.

Gebreyes. R. Women's march organisers address intersectionality as the movement grows. *Huffington Post.* 27, Jan 2017.

Gillborn, D. (2005). Education policy as an act of white supremacy: Whiteness, critical race theory and education reform. *Journal of education policy.* 20 (4).

Giroux, H. (2012). *Disposable youth: Racialized memories and the culture of cruelty.* New York and London: Routledge.

Giroux, H. (2001). *Theory and resistance in education: Towards a pedagogy for the opposition.* Westport, Connecticut: Bergin & Garvey.

Gordon, L. R. (2022). *Fear of Black consciousness.* UK: Penguin Random House.

Gordon, L. R. (2013). *Existentia Africana: Understanding Africana Existential Thought.* New York and London: Routledge.

Gordon, L. R. (2004). Critical Reflections on Three Popular Tropes in the Study of Whiteness. In *What White Looks Like* (pp. 189-210). Routledge.

Grande, S. (2009) Red pedagogy: Indigenous theories of redistribution. In Apple,M.A., Au W., & Gandin, L.A. *The routledge international handbook of critical education.*(pp.190-203). New York: Routledge Taylor and Francis Group.

Greene, M. (1988). *The dialectic of freedom.* New York: Teachers College Press.

Gusa, D.L. (2010). White institutional presence: The impact of whiteness on campus climate. *Harvard Educational Review.* 80(4). 464-489.

Hamad, R. (2020). *White tears/brown scars: How white feminism betrays women of color.* Australia; Catapult.

Hau Taki Haere| Tertiary Update (12 March, 2024). *Racism in the tertiary education sector.* 28 (4).

Harris, A. (2021). The GOP's 'critical race theory' obsession: How conservative polititicans and pundits became fixated on an academic approach. *The Atlantic.* 8, May 2021.

Harris, C. I. (1993). Whiteness as property. *Harvard Law Review,* 1707-1791. https://doi.org/10.2307/1341787

Harris, R., Tobias, M., Jeffreys, M., Waldegrave, K., Karlsen, S., & Nazroo, J. (2006). Effects of self-reported racial discrimination and deprivation on Māori health and inequalities in New Zealand: cross-sectional study. *The Lancet, 367*(9527), 2005-2009.

Haviland,V.S. (2008)."Things get glossed over": Rearticulating the silencing power of whiteness in education. *Journal of Teacher Education,* 59(1), 40–54.

Hedvah, J. (2020). *Sick woman theory.* https://www.kunstverein-hildesheim.de/assets/bilder/caring-structures-ausstellung-digital/Johanna-Hedva/cb6ec5c75f/AUSSTELLUNG_1110_Hedva_SWT_e.pdf.

Hill P. H (1998). *Fighting words: Black women and the search for justice.* Minneapolis: University of Minnesota Press.

Hincy, P.H. (2008). *Becoming a critical educator: Defining a classroom identity, designing a critical pedagogy.* New York: Peter Lang Publishing.

Hoskins, T.K. & Jones, A. (14, April 2023). Indigenising our universities. *E-tangata.co.nz*

hooks, b. (1994). *Teaching to transgress: Education as the practice of freedom.* New York. Routledge.

hooks, b. (1989). *Talking back: Thinking feminist, thinking black.* Boston, MA: South End Press.

hooks, b. (1986). Sisterhood: Political solidarity between women. *Feminist review.* 23, pp. 125-138.

Huber, L.P & Cueva, B.M. (2012). Chicana/Latina testimonios on effects and responses to microaggressions. *Equity and excellence in education,* 45(3), 392-410.

Huerta-Charles, L. (2007) Pedagogy of testimony: Reflections on the pedagogy of critical pedagogy. In McLaren, P. & Kincheloe, J.L. *Critical pedagogy: Where are we now?*. (pp.250-261). New York: Peter Lang.

Hydra Lernaia- https://www.theoi.com/Ther/DrakonHydra.html

Ings, W. (2017). *Disobedient teaching: Surviving and creating change in education.* Dunedin, NZ: Otago University Press.

I, too, am Auckland (2015). Mediacentre, maramatanga.ac.nz

Jackson, M. (2019). *The connection between white supremacy and colonisation.* E-Tangata. Retrieved from https://e-tangata.co.nz/comment-and-analysis/the-connection-between-white-supremacy/

Jackson, M. (2016). *Moana Jackson: Facing the truth about the wars.* E-Tangata. Retrieved from https://e-tangata.co.nz/history/moana-jackson-facing-the-truth-about-the-wars/.

Jacobson, M.F. (1998). *Whiteness of a different color: European immigrants and the alchemy of race.* Cambridge, MA: Harvard University Press.

Jayakumar, U. M. & Adamian, A. S. (2017). The fifth frame of colorblind ideology: Maintaining the comforts of colorblindness in the context of white fragility. *Sociological Perspectives, 60*(5), 912-936.

Johnson, A. and Joseph-Salisbury, R. (2018). "Are you supposed to be in here?" Racial microaggressions and knowledge production in higher education. (pp.143-160). In Jones, A. (2001). Cross-cultural pedagogy and the passion for ignorance. *Feminism and Psychology, 11*(30), pp. 279-292).

Kahi, R. (2022). *No Māori Allowed.* TVNZ.

Kelley, R., & Yancy, G. (2022, May 5). White indifference is normalising spectacular acts of violence. *Truthout.* https://truthout.org/articles/robin-kelley-white-indifference-is-normalizing-spectacular-acts-of-violence/

Khatun, as cited in Silverstein, J. (2017). Intersectionality, resistance, and history- making: A conversation between Carolyn D'Cruz, Ruth DeSouza, Samia Khatun, and Crystal McKinnon. *Lilith: A Feminist History Journal, 23,* 15–22

Kidman J. (2019). Whither decolonisation? Indigenous scholars and the problem of inclusion in the neoliberal university. *Journal of Sociology.* 2020;56(2):247-262. doi:10.1177/1440783319835958

Kidman, J.& Chu, C. (2019). "We're not the hottest ethnicity": Pacific scholars and the cultural politics of New Zealand universities. *Globalisation, Societies and Education, 17*(4), 489-499.

Kincheloe, J.K. and Steinberg, S.R. (2008). Indigenous knowledges in education: Complexities, dangers, and profound benefits. In Denzin, N.K. , Lincoln, Y.S. & Smith, L.T. *Handbook of critical and indigenous methodologies.* (pp.135-157). Los Angeles: Sage Publications.

Kincheloe, J.K. (2009). Contextualizing the madness: A critical analysis of the assault on teacher education and schools. In Groenke, S.L. & Hatch, J.A. *Critical pedagogy and teacher education in the neoliberal era, Small openings.* (pp.19-36). Springer Science.

Kinefuchi, E. & Orbe, M. P. (2008). Situating oneself in racialized world: Understanding student reactions to Crash through standpoint theory and context-positionality frame. *Journal of International and Intercultural Communication, 1*(1), 70-90.

Kluttz, J., Walker, J., & Walter, P. (2020). Unsettling allyship, unlearning and learning towards decolonising solidarity. *Studies in the Education of Adults, 52*(1), 49-66.

Knittel, M. (2018). *Making the Transition from Ally to Co-conspirator.* Medium. Retrieved from https://medium.com/@knit0371/making-the-transition-from-ally-to-co-conspirator-cc28a5752af7

Kumashiro, K.K. (2010). Seeing the bigger picture: Troubling movements to end teacher education. *Journal of Teacher Education.* 61 (1-2), 56-65.

Kusmashiro, K. (2012). *Bad teacher: How blaming teachers distorts the bigger picture.* New York: Teachers College Press.

Labaree, D.F. (1997). Public goods, private goods: The American struggle over educational goals. *American Educational Research Journal,* 34(1), 39-81.

Ladson-Billings, G. (2009). Race still matters: Critical race theory in education. (pp.110-122). In Apple, M.A., Au W., & Gandin, L.A. *The Routledge international handbook of critical education.* New York: Routledge Taylor and Francis Group.

Ladson-Billings, G. (2006). From the achievement gap to the education debt: Understanding achievement in U.S. schools. *Educational Researcher, 35*(7), 3-12.

Lather, P. (1991) *Getting smart: Feminist research and pedagogy with/in the postmodern.* New York: Routledge.

Leonardo, Z. (2017).White historical activity theory: Toward a critical understanding of white zones of proximal development. *Race and Ethnicity in Education,* 20(1), pp.15–29.

Leonardo, Z. (2015). Contracting race: writing, racism, and education. *Critical Studies in Education, 56*(1), 86-98.

Leonardo, Z. (2009). Pale/ontology: The status of whiteness in education. In Apple, M.A., Au, W., & Gandin, L.A. (eds) *The Routledge international handbook of critical education* (pp. 123–136). New York: Routledge Taylor and Francis Group.

Lewis, A.E. (2004). "What group?" Studying whites and whiteness in the era of "color-blindness". *Sociological Theory.* 22(4).pp. 623-646.

Lipman, P. (2016). School closings: The nexus of white supremacy, state abandonment, and accumulation by dispossessions. In Picower, B. & Mayorga, E. (2016). *What's race got to do with it? How current school reform policy maintains racial and economic inequality.* Peter Lang: New York.

Lipman, P. (2011). Neoliberal education restructuring. Dangers and opportunities of the present crisis. *Monthly review,* July/August; 3(63), pp. 114-127.

Lipsitz, G. (2019). The sounds of silence: How race neutrality preserves white supremacy.pp 23-51. In Crenshaw, K., Harris, L.C., HoSang, D.M. & Lipsitz, G.

(2109). *Seeing race again: Countering colorblindess across the disciplines.* Oakland: University of California Press.

Lorde, A. (1984). *Sister outsider: Essays and speeches.* Berkeley, CA: Crossing Press.

Matias, C.E. & Mackey, J. (2016). Breakin' down whiteness in antiracist teaching: Introducing critical whiteness pedagogy. *Urban Review.* 48: 32-50.

McAllister, T. G., Kidman, J., Rowley, O., & Theodore, R. F. (2019). Why isn't my Professor Māori? A snapshot of the academic workforce in New Zealand universities. *MAI Journal, 8*(2), 235-249.

McConville, A., Wetherell, M., McCreanor, T., Borell, B. & Barnes, H.M. (2019). 'Pissed off and confused'/grateful and (re)moved.' Affect privilege, and national commemoration in Aotearoa New Zealand. *Political psychology,* 41 (1) pp. 129-144.

McHugh, N. (2015). Keeping the strange unfamiliar: The racial privilege of dismantling whiteness. Pp. 141-153. In Yancy, G. (2015). *White self-criticality beyond anti-racism: How does it feel to be a white problem?* Lexington Books: New York.

McIntosh, P. (1990). White privilege: Unpacking the invisible knapsack. *Independent School,* 90(49), pp. 31–36.

McIntyre, A. (2002). Exploring whiteness and multicultural education with prospective teachers. *Curriculum Inquiry, 32*(1), 32-49.

Medina, J. (2019). Racial violence, emotional friction, and epistemic activism. *Angelaki, Journal of the Theoretical Humanities.* 24(4). Pp. 22-37.

Memmi, A. (1965). *The colonizer and the colonized.* Boston: The Orion Press, Inc.

Menchú, R. (1983). *I, Rigoberta Menchu An Indian woman in Guatemala.* London: Verso.

Ministry of Education. (2022, March 21). *Aotearoa New Zealand's histories and Te Takanga o Te Wā.* https://www.education.govt.nz/our-work/changes-in-education/aotearoa-new-zealands-histories-and-te-takanga-o-te-wa/

Million, D. (2009). Felt theory: An indigenous feminist approach to affect and history. *Wicazo SA Review.* (pp. 53-76).

Mills, C.W. (2015). The racial contract revisited: Still unbroken after all these years. *Politics, Groups, and Identities.* 3(3) 541-557.

Mills, C. W. (2007). White ignorance. In S. Sullivan. & N. Tuana (Eds.). *Race and Epistemologies of Ignorance.* Pp. 13-38. Albany: State University of New York Press.

Mills, C. W. (1997). *The racial contract.* New York: Cornell University Press.

Mohanty, C. T. (2013). Transnational feminist crossings: On neoliberalism and radical critique. *Signs, 38*(4). Pp. 967–991. https://doi.org/10.1086/669576

Moll, L. C., Amanti, C., Neff, D., & Gonzalez, N. (1992). Funds of knowledge for teaching: Using a qualitative approach to connect homes and classrooms. Theory into Practice, 31, 132-141. doi:10.1080/00405849209543534

Morrison, T. (1992). *Playing in the dark: Whiteness and the literary imagination.* New York: Vintage Books.

Move to End Violence. (2016, September 7). *Ally or Co-conspirator?* Move to End Violence. https://movetoendviolence.org/blog/ally-co-conspirator-means-act-insolidarity/

Muñoz, J.E. (2009). *Cruising utopia: The then and now of queer futurity.* New York and London: New York University Press.

Muñoz, and Noboa. 2018. "Hijacks and Hijinks on the US History Review Committee." In *Radical Educators-Rearticulating Education and Social Change: Teacher Agency and Resistance, Early 20th Century to the Present,* edited by Author and T. Y. Gourd, 117-133. New York, NY, and London, UK: Routledge.

Naepi, S. (2019). Why isn't my professor Pasifika? A snapshot of the academic workforce in New Zealand universities. *MAI Journal (Online),* 8(2), 219–234. https://doi.org/10.20507/MAIJournal.2019.8.2.9

Nayak, A (2007). Critical whiteness studies. *Sociology Compass.* 1(2) pp. 737-755.

Norris, A., de Saxe, J. & Cooper, G. (2023). Donna Awatare on whiteness in New Zealand: Theoretical contributions and contemporary relevance. *Decolonization of Criminology and Justice.* 5 (2). Pp. 1-20.

Norris, A. (2019). Discussing contemporary racial justice in academic spaces: Minimizing epistemic exploitation while neutralizing white fragility. In *The Palgrave Handbook of Ethnicity.* Palgrave Macmillan, Singapore. doi:10.1007/978-981-13-0242-8_162-1

Orange, C. (2012). 'Treaty of Waitangi', Te Ara – the Encyclopedia of New Zealand. Retrieved 4 February, 2022, from https://teara.govt.nz/en/treaty-of-waitangi.

Orozco, R., & Jaime Diaz, J. (2016). "Suited to their needs": White innocence as a vestige of segregation. *Multicultural Perspectives,* 18(3), 127-133.

Ovink, S.M. & Murrell, O.G. (2022). University diversity projects and the inclusivity challenge. *Socius: Sociological Research for a Dynamic World.* 8, 1-15.

Partnoy, A. (2003). On being shorter: How our testimonial texts defy the academy. In Hernandez, J. B. *Women writing resistance: Essays on Latin America and the Caribbean* (173-192). Cambridge, MA: South End Press.

Patel, L. (2015). Desiring diversity and backlash: White property rights in higher education. *Urban Review.* 47. 657-675.

Penehira, M., Green, A., Smith, L.T., & Aspin, C. (2014). Maori and Indigenous views on resistance and resilience. *Mai Journal,* 3(2), 97–110, at p. 97.

Pérez Huber, L. (2009). Disrupting apartheid of knowledge: testimonio as methodology in Latina/o critical race research in education. *International Journal of Qualitative Studies in Education,* 22(6), 639-654.

Perry, P. & Shotwell, A. (2009). Relational understanding and white anti-racist praxis. *Sociological Theory.* 27 (1).

Petersen-Smith, K., and Bean, B. (2015, May 14). *Fighting Racism and the Limits of "Ally-ship"*. Socialist Worker. https://socialistworker.org/2015/05/14/fighting -racism-and-the-limits-of-allyship

Picower, B. & Mayorga, E. (2016). *What's race got to do with it? How current school reform policy maintains racial and economic inequality*. New York: Peter Lang.

Pollock, M., Deckman, S., Mira, M., & Shalaby, C. (2009). "But what can I do?": Three necessary tensions in teaching teachers about race. *Journal of Teacher Education*, 61(3), pp. 211–224.

Quick, K. & Kahlenberg, R.D. (2019). Attacking the black-white opportunity gap that comes from residential segregation. *The century foundation*. 25, June 2019.

Reyes, K.B. & Rodríguez, J.E.C. (2012): Testimonio: Origins, terms, and resources. *Equity & Excellence in Education*, 45(3), 525-538.

Richards, T. (17, May 2020). The land of the wrong white crowd: Growing up and living in The shadow of racism. *E-Tangata*.

Rollock, N. (2018). The heart of whiteness: Racial gesture politics, equity and higher education. Pp. 313-330. In Arday, J., & Mirza, H. S. (2018). *Dismantling Race in Higher Education: Racism, Whiteness and Decolonising the Academy*. Springer International Publishing AG. https://doi.org/10.1007/978-3-319-60261-5

Ross, L. (2010). *Inventing the savage: The social construction of Native American criminality*. University of Texas Press.

Ross, W. (2017). The fear created by precarious existence in the neoliberal world discourages critical thinking. Retrieved from the *American Herald Tribune*. Interview by Mohsen Abdelmoumen.

Saavedera, C.M & Pérez, M. S. (2012): Chicana and Black feminisms: Testimonios of theory, identity, and multiculturalism. *Equity & Excellence in Education*. 45(3), 430-443.

Salomona, R.P, Portelli, J.P., Daniel, B-J., & Campbell, A. (2006). The discourse of denial: How white teacher candidates construct race, racism and 'white privilege'. *Race, Ethnicity and Education*. 8(2), 147-169.

Sandoval, C. (2000). *Methodology of the oppressed*. Minneapolis: University of Minnesota Press.

Satherly, D. (2021, June 5). *Education Minister Chris Hipkins not a fan of the phrase 'white privilege', but acknowledges it exists*. Newshub.

Seidl, B .L. & Hancock, S. D. (2011). Acquiring double images: White preservice teachers locating themselves in a raced world. *Harvard Educational Review*, 81(4), 687-709.

Silverstein, J. (2017). Intersectionality, resistance, and history-making: A conversation between Carolyn D'Cruz, Ruth DeSouza, Samia Khatun, and Crystal McKinnon. *Lilith; A Feminist History Journal*, 23, 15-22.

Simmonds, N. (2011). Mana wahine: Decolonising politics. *Women's Studies Journal*, 25(2), pp. 11–25.

Smith, A., Funaki, H. & MacDonald (2021). Living, breathing settler-colonialism: The reification of settler norms in common university space. *Higher Education Research & Development.* 40 (1) pp. 132-145.

Smith, H., Le Grice, J., Fonua, S., & Mayeda, D. (2022). Coloniality, institutional racism and white fragility: A *wero* to higher education. *The Australian journal of Indigenous education.* 51 (2). DOI10.55146/ajie.v51i2.34

Solorzano, D. G., & Yosso, T. J. (2009). Critical race methodology: Counter-storytelling as an analytical framework from educational research. In E. Taylor, D. Gillborn, & G. Ladson-Billings (Eds.), Foundations of critical race theory in education (pp. 340–348). New York, NY: Routledge.

Solnit, R. (2016). *Hope in the dark: Untold histories, wild possibilities.* Chicago: Haymarket Books, xxv.

Spring, J. (1996). *American education (7th ed.).* New York: McGraw-Hill Inc.

Spring, J. (1988). *Conflicts of interest: The politics of American education.* London: Longman.

Steele, C. M. (1997). A threat in the air: How stereotypes shape intellectual identity and performance. *American Psychologist, 52*(6), 613–629.

Stewart, G.T. (2023). Truth-myths of New Zealand. *AJPH* 2, 5, 1-16. https://doi.org/10.1007/s44204-022-00059-7

Stewart, G. T., MacDonald, L., Matapo, J., Fa'avae, D. T. M., Watson, B. K., Akiu, R. K., Martin, B., Mika, C., & Sturm, S. (2023). Surviving academic Whiteness: Perspectives from the Pacific. *Educational Philosophy and Theory, 55*(2), 141–152. https://doi.org/10.1080/00131857.2021.2010542

Stewart, G. T. (2020). A typology of Pākehā "Whiteness" in education. *Review of Education, Pedagogy, and Cultural Studies, 42*(4), 296-310.

Storch, E. A. & Storch, J. B (2003). Academic dishonesty and attitudes towards academic dishonest acts: Support for cognitive dissonance theory. *Psychological Reports, 92,* 174-176.

Straus, V. How 'segrenomics' underpins the movement to privatize public education. *Washington Post. 19 January 2018.*

Strmic-Pawl, H.V. (2015). More than a knapsack: The white supremacy flower as a new model for teaching racism. *Sociology of Race and Ethnicity.*1(1), pp. 192-197.

Sue, D.W., Capodilupo, C.M., Nadal, K.L., & Torino, G.C. (2008). Racial microaggressions and the power to define reality. *American Psychologist, 63* (4), 277-279.

Suissa, J. (2010). *Anarchism and education: A philosophical perspective.* Oakland: PM Press, Teaching Council of Aotearoa New Zealand. (2021). *Unteach Racism.* https://www.unteachracism.nz/

Tecun, A., Lopesi, L. & Sankar, A. (Eds). (2022). *Towards a grammar of race in Aotearoa, New Zealand.* Wellington, NZ: Bridget Williams Books.

Teel, K (2105). Feeling white, feeling good: "Antiracist" white sensibilities. Pp. 37-57. In Yancy, G. (2015). *White self-criticality beyond anti-racism: How does it feel to be a white problem?* Lexington Books: New York.

Tervalon, M., & Murray-Garcia, J. (1998). Cultural humility versus cultural competence: A critical distinction in defining physician training outcomes in multicultural education, *Journal of Health Care for the Poor and Underserved* 9(2),117-125.

Thomas, J.M. (2018). Diversity regimes and racial inequality: A case study of diversity university. *Social Currents*. 5(2). 140-156.

Tuari Steward, G., MacDonald, L., Matapo, J., Taufui Mikato Fa'avae, D., Ka'imi Watson, B., Kahikuonalani Akiu, R., Martin, B., Mika, C. & Sturm, S. (2023). Surviving acadmic whiteness: Perspectives from the Pacific. *Educational Philosophy and Theory*. 55 (2), pp. 141-152.

Tuhiwai Smith, L. (1999). *Decolonizing methodologies:* Research and indigenous peoples. London: University of Otago Press.

Twine, F.W. & Gallagher, C. (2008). The future of whiteness: a map of the 'third wave'. *Ethnic and Racial Studies. 31(1).* 4-24.

Tyack, D. (2003). *Seeking common ground: Public schools in a diverse society.* Massachusetts: Harvard University Press.

Villenas, S. A. (2019). Pedagogies of being with: Witnessing, testimonio, and critical love in everyday social movement. *International Journal of Qualitative Studies in Education, 32*(2), 151–166. https://doi.org/10.1080/095 18398.2018.1533148

Walker, A. (1983). In search of our mothers' gardens: womanist prose. San Diego: Harcourt Brace Jovanovich.

Warikoo, N.K. & de Novais, J. (2015). Colour-blindness and diversity: Race frames and their consequences for white undergraduates at elite US universities. *Ethnic and Racial Studies*. 38 (6), 860-876.

Watson, D. (2014). Staying in the conversation. Having difficult conversations about race in teacher education. In G. Yancy (Ed.). *Exploring race in predominantly white classrooms* (pp. 40-49). New York: Routledge.

White, E. (2012). Whiteness and teacher education. New York: Routledge.

Wilkerson, I. (2020). *Caste; The lies that divide us.* UK: Penguin Random House.

Yancy, G. (14 March, 2023). Interview-Adele Norris: Anti-Black Racism Is Global. So Must Be the Movement to End It. *Truthout.org*

Yancy, G. (5 May, 2022). Interview-Robin Kelley: White indifference is normalising spectacular acts of violence. *Truthout.org*

Yancy, G. (2018). *Backlash: What Happens When We Talk Honestly about Racism in America?* Maryland: Rowman & Littlefield.

Yancy, G. (2015). *White self-criticality beyond anti-racism: How does it feel to be a white problem?* Lexington Books: New York.

Yancy, G. (2012). *Look, a white! Philosophical essays on whiteness.* Philadelphia: Temple University Press.

Yosso, T. J., Smith, W. A., Ceja, M., & Solorzano, D. G. (2010). Critical race theory, racial microaggressions, and campus racial climate for Latina/o undergraduates. *Harvard Educational Review,* 79(4) 659-690.

Yosso, T.J. (2006). *Critical Race Counterstories along the Chicana/Chicano Educational Pipeline,* Ch. 4-undergraduates.

Yudice, G. (1991). Testimonio and postmodernism: Whom does testimonial writing represent? *Latin American Perspectives,* 18 (3)15-31.

Zakaria, R. (2021). *Against white feminism.* Penguin Books: United Kingdom.

Zamalin, A. (2019). Ida. B. Wells: The anti-lynching movement and the politics of seeing. In *Struggle on their minds: The political thought of African American resistance.*

Index

www.ingramcontent.com/pod-product-compliance
Lightning Source LLC
Chambersburg PA
CBHW050513280326
41932CB00014B/2304